The Psalm Locator,

EDITED BY ANTHONY LAWRENCE

Published by
Resource Publications, Inc.
160 E. Virginia St. #290
San Jose, CA 95112

Copyright Acknowledgements

Psalm 47:6-7 from *The New English Bible*, ©The Delegates of the Oxford University Press and The Syndics of the Cambridge University Press, 1961, 1970. Used with the publisher's permission.

Adaptation of Psalm 96 ©1975 by Catherine de Vinck. "Renew My Spirit" from *A Book of Uncommon Prayers*, ©1976 by Catherine de Vinck. Alleluia Press, Box 103, Allendale, NJ 07401. Used with the publisher's permission.

Quotation from *Out Of The Depths* by Bernhard W. Anderson. ©1970, 1974 Bernhard W. Anderson. Used by permission of the Westminster Press.

"Dead Letter" from *At Times I See*, by Huub Oosterhuis. ©1974 by The Seabury Press. Used with the publisher's permission.

"Seeking God's Name" and "Of This Earth" from *Your Word Is Near*, by Huub Oosterhuis. ©1968 by The Paulist Press. Used with the publisher's permission.

Excerpts from *The Jerusalem Bible*, ©1966 by Darton, Longman & Todd, Ltd. and Doubleday & Company, Inc. Used with the publisher's permission.

Psalm 150 from *Lyric Psalms: Half a Psalter*, by Francis Patrick Sullivan. ©1983 National Association of Pastoral Musicians. Used with the publisher's permission.

Editorial Director: Kenneth Guentert
Production Editor: Scott Alkire
Mechanical Layout: Geoff Rogers and Agnes Hou
Cover Design: Agnes Hou

ISBN 0-89390-085-0
Library of Congress Catalog Card Number 86-060174
Printed and bound in the United States 5 4 3 2 1

Contents

1. Preface 1

2. How to Use the Listing 3

3. Why Do We Sing the Psalms? 5

4. The Listing 8

5. Responsorial Psalm Index for the Sundays
   and Holydays of the Year 102

6. Listing of Publishers 104

7. Snging the Psalms in Liturgies 106

8. Annotated Bibliography 114

9. Psalms to List? 116

10. Postscript 117

   Creative Adaptions and Examples:
   Dead Letter (Psalm 13) 14
   Adaptation of Psalm 55 40
   Renew My Spirit (Psalm 55) 42
   Adaptation of Psalm 96 66
   Psalm 150 98
   Seeking God's Name 110

Preface

This book is principally a listing of songs based on the book of Psalms of the Hebrew Bible. It is a planning aid, useful for selecting music for liturgies, services, prayer meetings or any gathering where a psalm may be sung. It contains lists of psalm-based songs from over forty publishers, and collections common in most Christian denominations such as Baptist, Episcopal, Lutheran and Methodist have been included, although the emphasis is on Roman Catholic sources.

The first edition, published in 1980, listed 1567 titles; for this second edition the list has been extended to almost 2300 titles. While part of the increase has come from searches of more hymnals and songbooks, those people who sent their personal lists to the publisher made a significant contribution. We want to thank them particularly; some of them went to great pains to help.

In the last four years there has been a significant decrease in the rate of publication of new liturgical music. One reason is that the national economy has been at an ebb, but another seems to be that the first wave of creativity caused by the liturgical renewals from the Second Vatican Council has run its course. We seem to have reached a consolidation phase; I think we are now more concerned with quality than quantity.

I hope you will find that this collection helps to bring out the ability of the psalms to speak to God for your community. Will you also help in the task of improving this book still further? Please use the "write-in" sheet at the end of the book to send in your own lists for inclusion in the next edition.

Anthony Lawrence

Sing lustily and with good courage. Beware of singing as if you were half dead, or half asleep; but lift up your voice with strength. Be no more afraid of your voice now, nor more ashamed of its being heard, than when you sung the songs of Satan.

Sing modestly. Do not bawl, so as to be heard above or distinct from the rest of the congregation, that you may not destroy the harmony; but strive to unite your voices together, so as to make one clear melodious sound.

Sing in time. Whatever time is sung be sure to keep with it. Do not run before nor stay behind it; but attend close to the leading voices, and move therewith as exactly as you can; and take care not to sing too slow. This drawling way naturally steals on all who are lazy; and it is high time to drive it out from us, and sing all our tunes just as quick as we did at first.

Above all sing spiritually. Have an eye to God in every word you sing. Aim at pleasing him more than yourself, or any other creature. In order to do this attend strictly to the sense of what you sing, and see that your heart is not carried away with the sound but offered to God continually; so shall your singing be such as the Lord will approve here, and reward you when he cometh in the clouds of heaven.

From John Wesley's preface to *Sacred Melody*, 1761

How to Use the Listing

In the following pages songs based on psalms have been listed under the psalm number. There are two numbering systems used today, the Hebrew and the Septuagint. The Hebrew is the original compilation of the psalms and the Septuagint is a Greek translation of the Scriptures made about 250 BCE.

Legend has it that about 70 Jewish translators were sent to Alexandria to provide a scripture for the use of the Greek-speaking Gentile world, hence *Septuagint* for seventy. Translation was accompanied by editing and the psalms were altered a little, such as by combining Hebrew numbered psalms 9 and 10. This put most of the Septuagint numbers one behind the Hebrew. The Protestant reformers reverted to the Hebrew numbering and today it is used by most scripture scholars. The Jerusalem, New American, New English and the Revised Standard (Common) bibles all use Hebrew numbering; the Grail translation is the most notable Septuagint version presently in use.

As Hebrew numbering is used in the listing, in a few instances the number given by a publisher may be one lower. Only numbered psalms from the Psalter have been listed; the songs in Exodus, Judges and so on have not been included. As psalms 14 and 53 are identical, the same entries have been put in both places. In the cases of psalms 70 and 108, which are made from parts of other psalms (70 is the same as 40:12-17 and 108 is the sum of 57:7-11 and 60:5-12) there is no cross listing. Songs on these psalms are listed under the number assigned by the publisher.

The listing provides a title if one is known; a blank means that the composer called the work "Psalm xx". Under Author the listing includes translators and arrangers, and when it is known the form is: words/music. Publishers are listed by the three-letter codes based on those in Resource Publication's *The Music Locator* and given on page 104 together with the publishers' addresses. Following the publisher code is a "source code" using the following initials:

Letter   Source

a   record album, disk

h   holograph, copy direct from author/publisher

m   magazine, e.g. *Modern Liturgy*

o   choral octavo

s   song book, hymnal

t   tape recording, cassette

If the song is part of a collection, the collection title is listed. The listing has been spaced such that you can write your own discoveries in the gaps. Also, the last page forms a "write-in" sheet for you to send additions to the publisher for inclusion in the next edition of this book.

Why Do We Sing the Psalms?

Generation after generation, people have discovered that in the trials of life the Sacred Scriptures contain the message that God remains with the world. The creator of the universe is far from an impersonal, uncaring being, or one who made us to be slaves. God is pictured as a loving parent who is deeply concerned for creation. All the books of the scriptures tell us this, but there is a unique book which not only speaks *to* us *of* God but speaks *for* us *to* God. This book is the Psalter and it speaks for us in our everyday humanity, in our depression, in our sickness, our fear, our delight at experiencing love and acceptance and our joy at the beauty of creation. It tells us that if we look back we can see God's hand guiding us, individually but more important as a community dedicated to living God's way.

The way of God as revealed to the Jews is preserved in the Torah, and

> *Happy is the one*
> *who never follows the advice of the wicked,*
> *or loiters on the way that sinners take,*
> *or sits around with scoffers*
> *but finds pleasure in the Law of God.*
>
> Psalm 1, after Jerusalem Bible

To the Christian, the Law has been made perfect in the way of Jesus, now proclaimed as "the way, the truth and the life." "And for anyone who is in Christ there is a new creation, the old creation is gone, and now the new one is here." (2 Cor. 5:17 JB) But the problems of living have not gone away in New Creation times, although the nature of the problems may have changed. In ancient Israel, raiding Philistines were a cause of lamentation which no longer concerns us today. Instead we live under the shadow of the wings of bombers carrying total vaporization in the form of nuclear bombs. It seems that when you get to the root of it, the lot of humanity is to struggle against its own greed, fear and ignorance.

This is the fundamental problem to which the opening chapters of the Bible are addressed: human grandeur and human misery, the high calling and the lost opportunity.

In our own time we can sense this human problem clearly as we see how science, which could be the form of imaging God's rule on earth, holds the terrifying possibility of nuclear destruction of the earth and of carrying military adventures into space. Moreover, we have been made painfully aware of the fact that human exploitation of the earth's resources may upset the balance of nature, with the result that the earth will no longer be a habitable place for human and animal life. The question is whether human beings— as scientists, industrialists, or technologists—can fulfill the high calling that was given to humanity by the Creator.

Anderson, *Out of the Depths*, 1983, p.155

While the psalms speak of the problems of living more than any other subject, they totally acknowledge God's presence and caring in the world. There is no "God is dead" feeling of despair even in the depths of lamentation, and there are over sixty psalms of lament. In Psalm 22: "My God, my God, why have you abandoned me?", recalled by the dying Jesus, the psalmist asks God to save him so that he may witness to God's mercy and sing God's praises to the whole assembly. Every psalm, whatever its type, praises and glorifies God.

The psalms were written over a period of some 700 years by many authors who submerged their identities and the specific details of their lives. They wrote of joy and agony, peace and misery in such a way that people have been able to asssociate with them in all the centuries since they were compiled.

What kind of experience awakens the impulse to praise God? To understand the answer is to get to the heart of the psalms. Can a person who has never been led from slavery, through a desert to a promised land sing with feeling:

The Lord is my light and my salvation:
whom shall I fear?
The Lord is the strength of my life:
of whom shall I be afraid?

Psalm 27

The Psalter includes songs of praise (hymns) and songs of thanksgiving. "Old Hundredth" (Psalm 100) is a well-known example of a hymn of praise and Psalm 136 is a song of thanksgiving. It is known as the Great Hallel:

Give thanks for the Lord is good,
for his love endures forever.
Give thanks to the God of gods,
for his love endures forever.
Give thanks to the Lord of lords,
for his love endures forever.

Grail Version

So we see that the psalms speak for us at our most human level, and so it is right that we should pray them both privately and publicly. Eucharistic liturgies place a psalm in the Liturgy of the Word to become a response to the message of the first reading — the message of God's intimacy with his people. The psalm is not an intellectual assent to an abstruse theological argument; it is an emotional expression. The psalmist does not argue like a rabbi but cries, touches and feels his love, suffering and rejoicing. He can honestly cry: "You were there then, God; where are you now?"

God, have you finally rejected us,
raging at the flock you used to pasture?
Rise, God, say something on your own behalf...

Psalm 74, JB

The whole people of God can pray these psalms, the pilgrim church beset on its journey by the "world" which sometimes appears to have no standards of honesty, justice, truth and love.

The Psalter is a songbook, that of the Second Temple in Jerusalem, and so psalms should usually be sung rather than recited in our liturgies, prayer meetings and other services. We have no idea of the original melodies of the Hebrew songs so we need to interpret them in translation in whatever way best serves to make them speak for us, in our time. There are many ways of singing psalms and there are important criteria for choosing the most appropriate way; these are discussed in the section entitled *Singing the Psalms in Liturgies*, page 106.

The Listing

1

Blessed Is The Man	Michael Baughen	GIA	s	Psalm Praise
Blessed Is The Man	Thomas Tallis	AUG	s	Psalms For The Church Year
Happy Are They	J. Coller	OSB	s	Benedictine Book Of Song
Happy Are They	Tim Schoenbachler	PAA	ast	All Is Ready
Happy Are They	Thompson/Gelineau	GIA	st	Gelineau Gradual
Happy Are They	P. Cunningham	GRA	ht	
Happy Are They	J. G. Phillips	WLP	s	Cantor Book
Happy Are They	Joe Zsigray	NAL	a	Berakah
Happy Indeed Is The Man	Joseph Gelineau	GIA	s	30 Psalms & 2 Canticles
Happy Is The Man	William Callahan	ACP	s	Song Leader's Handbook
Happy Man	Gregory Norbet	WES	ast	Winter's Coming Home
Happy The Man	E. Wittig	GRA	st	Cast Into The Deep
How Happy Is The Man	S. Somerville	WLP	s	Psalms For Singing,Bk.1
Praise The Lord For He Is Good	Douglas Mews	GIA	s	ICEL Lectionary Music
The Man Is Ever Blest	Isaac Watts	CON	s	The Lutheran Hymnal
The Righteous Ones	Thai Folk Hymn	MPH	s	The Book Of Hymns
Tree Of Life	Suzanne Toolan	RPB	ast	Keeping Festival
Your Word O Lord	C. B. Garve	AUG	s	Lutheran Book Of Worship

2

Battle Hymn Of The Republic	Julia Ward Howe	ACP	s	The Johannine Hymnal
Christ Is Our Leader		ACP	s	The Johannine Hymnal
The Lord Said To Me	Joe Wise	PAA	a	Hand In Hand
This Is My Son	Willard Jabusch	WLP	as	We Have Seen His Star
Why Do The Heathen Conspire?	Baughen/Thornton	GIA	s	Psalm Praise
Why This Tumult?	Joseph Gelineau	GIA	s	24 Psalms & A Canticle

3

Here I Am, Send Me	Tim Schoenbachler	PAA	a	All Is Ready
How Many Are My Foes	Joseph Gelineau	GIA	s	Grail-Gelineau Psalter
Now The Light Has Gone	F. Havergal	CON	s	The Lutheran Hymnal
Song Of Trust	Ron Ellis	NAL	ast	Starlight
Through The Day	Kelly/J. C. Bach	CON	s	The Lutheran Hymnal

4

Give Me An Answer	F. Hillebrand	AHC	ast	Long Way Home
Halay, When To God I Send	Paul Quinlan	FEL	s	Hymnal For Young Christians
Know That The Lord	Westendorf/Takacs	WLP	s	People's Mass Book
Lead Me Lord	Samuel Wesley	MPH	s	The Book Of Hymns
Let Your Face Shine Upon Us	Marty Haugen	PAA	ast	With Open Hands
Lord Let Your Face Shine	P. Cunningham	GRA	ht	
Lord Let Your Face Shine On Us	Angelo Della Picca	WLP	s	Cantor Book
Lord Let Your Face Shine On Us	Batastini/Gelineau	GIA	st	Gelineau Gradual
O Righteous Lord	Wilson/Wilson	GIA	s	Psalm Praise
When I Call	Joseph Gelineau	GIA	s	30 Psalms & 2 Canticles
When I Call	William Callahan	ACP	s	Song Leader's Handbook
When I Call Out	S. Somerville	WLP	s	Psalms For Singing, Bk.1

5

Heed My Call For Help	John Foley	NAL	as	Neither Silver Nor Gold
Help Me Know The Way	Paul Quinlan	WLP	a	Glory Bound
Lead Me Lord	Samuel Wesley	MPH	s	The Book Of Hymns
Lord, In The Morning	Watts/Stanley	HOP	s	The Service Hymnal
O Blessed Holy Trinity	Behm,Schuette/Herman	CON	s	The Lutheran Hymnal
Redeemer King		ACP	s	The Johannine Hymnal
To My Words Give Ear	Joseph Gelineau	GIA	s	20 Psalms & 3 Canticles

6

	Schutz/Reuning	GIA	s	The Becker Psalter
How Can You Really Care?	Paul Quinlan	NAL	a	It's A Brand New Day
Lord, Do Not Reprove Me	Joseph Gelineau	GIA	s	Grail-Gelineau Psalter
O Lord Be Gracious	Perry/Warren	GIA	s	Psalm Praise
O Faithful God	Selnecker	CON	s	The Lutheran Hymnal

7

God Who Madest Earth	Albert, Winkworth	CON	s	The Lutheran Hymnal
In God, My Faithful God	Weingartner	CON	s	The Lutheran Hymnal
O Lord God, I Take Refuge	Joseph Gelineau	GIA	s	Grail-Gelineau Psalter

8

Psalm 8	A. Frankenpohl	BBL		
Psalm 8	Edwin Fissinger	WLP	s	Three Sacred Anthems
Psalm 8	Isadore Freed	SOM		
All My Days	Murray/Schutte	NAL	as	Neither Silver Nor Gold
All My Days	Murray/Schutte	NAL	st	Glory And Praise,1
Charlotte's Song	Tom Parker	WLP	a	Let All The Earth Sing
Forever, O Lord	J. H. Maunder	PRO		
How Glorious Is Your Name	Howard Hughes	RPB	st	Gather 'Round, Too
How Glorious Is Your Name	Eugene Englert	GIA	o	
How Great Is Your Name	James Hansen	GIA	o	
How Great Is Your Name	Tobias Colgan	ABB	ast	Songs Like Incense
How Great Is Your Name	Joseph Gelineau	GIA	s	Worship II
How Great Is Your Name	Joseph Gelineau	GIA	s	24 Psalms & A Canticle
How Great Is Your Name	C.Knoll/F.V.Strahan	HEL	s	The Catholic Liturgy Book
O Lord Our God	Michael Baughen	GIA	s	Psalm Praise
O Lord Our God How Great	John B. Dykes	ACP	s	The Johannine Hymnal
O Lord, How Great Is Your Name	Paul Quinlan	WLP	a	Glory Bound
O Lord, Our God	M.Shepherd/R.Hillert	AUG	s	Seasonal Psalms
O Lord, Our God	Richard Hillert	AUG	o	
O Lord, Our God	Betty Pulkingham	RPB	m	Modern Liturgy,10.5
O Lord, Our God	Betty Pulkingham	RPB	t	You Are My Witnesses
O Lord, Our God	Carroll/Gelineau	GIA	st	Gelineau Gradual
O Lord, Our God	H. H. Smith	WLP	s	Cantor Book
O Lord, Our God	Anon/Vulpius	MPH	s	The Book Of Hymns
O How Glorious	Curtis Beech	PIL	s	Pilgrim Hymnal
O How Glorious	Beech/Beethoven	MPH	s	The Book Of Hymns
When I Behold	William Callahan	ACP	s	Song Leader's Handbook
Yahweh Our Lord How Wonderful	S. Somerville	WLP	s	Psalms For Singing,Bk.1
Your Name, O Lord	Joe Zsigray	NAL	as	Sing A Song Of Love

9

I Will Praise You Lord	Joseph Gelineau	GIA	s	Grail-Gelineau Psalter
Rise Up O Lord Our God	William H. Walter	ACP	s	The Johannine Hymnal

10

| In My Hour Of Grief | Dudley-Smith/Baughen | GIA | s | Psalm Praise |
| Lord, Why Do You Stand Afar? | Joseph Gelineau | GIA | s | Grail-Gelineau Psalter |

11

| In The Lord I Have Taken | Joseph Gelineau | GIA | s | Grail-elineau Psalter |
| Run Like A Deer | Paul Quinlan | FEL | s | Hymnal For Young Christians |

12

Father of Mercy	Owen Alstott/Randall D		s	Choral Praise—1985
Help, O Lord	Joseph Gelineau	GIA	s	Grail-Gelineau Psalter
O Lord Look Down	Martin Luther	CON	s	The Lutheran Hymnal

13

Psalm 13	Robert Baksa	SOM		
Even Then	Oosterhuis/Huijbers	NAL	as	When From Our Exile
Forgotten For Eternity	Saward/Wilson	GIA	s	Psalm Praise
How Long, O Lord	Joseph Gelineau	GIA	s	Grail-Gelineau Psalter
How Long, O Lord	Paul Quinlan	WLP	a	Glory Bound
The Day Is Past	Neale/Brown	CON	s	The Lutheran Hymnal

Dead Letter

How much longer?
Have you simply banished me from your thoughts?
No?
But you sure try.
I hear you're doing badly,
that you're nowhere.
How long will you go on
avoiding me
or passing by in disguise
or not answering when I phone
not opening when I knock?

Must that go on,
this discord in my soul
this suffocating doubt—
never again...but still?
And the neighbors and our close friends
who know about us
just laugh and say
"him and his God!"
While people treat me
like gods, still
no word from you, and even
this letter is not deliverable.
And some fine day
we're going to die, with a plop
or slowly of a tumor
or drift away in sleep.
Standing over me
that single foe shall bend,
the deadly enemy.
I'll feel his breath
upon my face
and then I'll barely hear him saying:
finally.

Even then I'll cling to you
whether you want me or not,
in your good grace
or out of it.
"Save me!" I'll cry out to you
or maybe only
"Love me."

Psalm 13, freely adapted
Huub Oosterhuis *At Times I See*
©1974 by The Seabury Press, NY

14 _____

The Fool Has Said	Joseph Gelineau	GIA	s	Grail-Gelineau Psalter

15 _____

He Who Does Justice	E. Diemente	WLP	s	Cantor Book
He Who Does Justice	Proulx/Gelineau	GIA	st	Gelineau Gradual
He Who Does Justice	P. Cunningham	GRA	ht	
He Who Walks	William Callahan	ACP	s	Song Leader's Handbook
Lord, Who May Stay	S. Somerville	WLP	s	Psalms For Singing,Bk.2
What Kind Of Man	Barnes/Wilson	GIA	s	Psalm Praise
Who Will Dwell	Paul Quinlan	WLP	a	Glory Bound
Yahweh, Who Can Enter	Helen Marie Gilsdorf	RPB	m	Modern Liturgy,8.6
Yahweh, Who Can Enter	Helen Marie Gilsdorf	RPB	at	In The Breaking Of Bread
You Are My Friends	Betty Pulkingham	RPB	m	Modern Liturgy,10.4
You Are My Friends	Betty Pulkingham	RPB	t	You Are My Witnesses

16

Psalm 16	Joseph Gelineau	GIA	s	20 Psalms & 3 Canticles
A Little Further	Paul Quinlan	WLP	a	Glory Bound
Abba, Father	Helen Marie Gilsdorf	RPB	st	Gather 'Round
For You Are My God	John Foley	NAL	st	Glory And Praise,1
For You Are My God	John Foley	NAL	as	Neither Silver Nor Gold
Forth In Thy Name, O Lord	Wesley/Gibbons	AUG	s	Lutheran Book Of Worship
Gifting Us	Ed Gutfreund	NAL	as	Harmonizing Word
God's Word Is Our Great Help	Grundtvig	CON	s	The Lutheran Hymnal
Great God A Blessing	Schuette/Cruger	AUG	s	Lutheran Book Of Worship
Keep Me O God	William Callahan	ACP	s	Song Leader's Handbook
Keep Me Safe	J. G. Phillips	WLP	s	Cantor Book
Keep Me Safe	Peloquin/Gelineau	GIA	st	Gelineau Gradual
Keep Me Safe	Robert Mondoy	RPB	st	Gather 'Round, Too
Keep Me Safe, O God	Dean Olawski	WRD	s	Give Thanks To The Lord
Keep Me Safe, O God	P. Cunningham	GRA	ht	
Lord You Will Show Us	Peloquin/Gelineau	GIA	st	Gelineau Gradual
Lord You Will Show Us	R. J. Schaffer	WLP	s	Cantor Book
O Lord My Allotted Portion	William Callahan	ACP	s	Song Leader's Handbook
O Trinity Most Blessed	St. Ambrose/Herman	CON	s	The Lutheran Hymnal
Path Of Life	Balhoff/Daigle Et Al.	NAL	as	Path Of Life
Preserve Me, O God	Joseph Gelineau	GIA	o	
Protect Me God	Saward/Strover	GIA	s	Psalm Praise
The Path Of Life	Rory Cooney	NAL	ast	You Alone
When All Your Mercies	Addison/Kirbye	AUG	s	Lutheran Book Of Worship
You Are My Inheritance	J. G. Phillips	WLP	s	Cantor Book
You Are My Inheritance	Thompson/Gelineau	GIA	st	Gelineau Gradual

17

Evening Air Psalm	M. Williamson	BOH		
Hear O Lord	William Callahan	ACP	s	Song Leader's Handbook
Lord When Your Glory Appears	Angelo Della Picca	WLP	s	Cantor Book
Lord When Your Glory Appears	Hughes/Gelineau	GIA	st	Gelineau Gradual
Lord, When Your Glory	P. Cunningham	GRA	ht	
Steadfast In Your Paths	P. Cunningham	GRA	ht	
The Cry Of The Poor	John Foley	NAL	s	Glory And Praise,2

18 _____

Christ Is Our Leader		ACP	s	The Johannine Hymnal
God The Father Be Our Stay	Luther/Walther	AUG	s	Lutheran Book Of Worship
God The Father Be Our Stay	Luther/Walther	CON	s	The Lutheran Hymnal
How Sweet The Name	Newton/Reinagle	AUG	s	Lutheran Book Of Worship
I Love You Lord My Strength	P. Cunningham	GRA	ht	
I Love You Lord My Strength	Proulx/Gelineau	GIA	st	Gelineau Gradual
I Love You Lord My Strength	Angelo Della Picca	WLP	s	Cantor Book
I Love You, Lord, My Strength	Jeffrey Keyes	RPB	mt	Modern Liturgy,11.7
I Love You O Lord	William Callahan	ACP	s	Song Leader's Handbook
I Will Call On The Lord	M. Williamson	BOH		
In You I Take Refuge	Dick Hillard	RPB	mt	Modern Liturgy,5.4
Lord Thee I Love	Schalling/Schmid	AUG	s	Lutheran Book Of Worship
Lord Thee I Love	Schalling	CON	s	The Lutheran Hymnal
Lowly People You Save	P. Cunningham	GRA	ht	
O Lord I Love You	Richard Bewes	GA	s	Psalm Praise
The Lord Is My Light	John Foley	NAL	as	A Dwelling Place
Yea, Thou Dost Light My Lamp	Jane Yankitis	WGM	s	Songs Of Praise,2

19 _____

Psalm 19	Edwin Fissinger	WLP	s	Three Sacred Anthems
Psalm 19	Tom Conry	NAL	at	Ashes
Drop Down Dew	Judy O'Sheil	FEL	s	Hymnal For Young Christians
Holy Majesty, Before You	Hedborn/Nicolai	AUG	s	Lutheran Book Of Worship
I Lift Up My Soul	Eugene Englert	AUG	o	
It's A Brand New Day	Paul Quinlan	WGM	as	Songs Of Praise,1
It's A Brand New Day	Paul Quinlan	NAL	s	Glory And Praise,2
Lord You Have The Word	Angelo Della Picca	WLP	o	
Lord You Have The Words	C. A. Peloquin	GIA	ao	Lyric Liturgy
Lord You Have The Words	Christopher Willcock	PAA	ot	Psalms For Feasts & Seasons
Lord You Have The Words	John Lee	OSB	s	Book Of Sacred Song
Lord You Have The Words	Proulx/Gelineau	GA	s	Gelineau Gradual
Lord You Have The Words	P. Cunningham	GRA	ht	
Lord You Have The Words	Richard Proulx	GIA	o	
Lord, You Have The Words	David Haas	GIA	s	Psalms For The Chruch Year
Lord, You Have The Words	Ralph C. Verdi	WLP	s	Psalms For The Cantor,1
Lord, You Have The Words	ichael Joncas	COO	ast	Every Stone Shall Cry
Most Perfect Is The Law	Hutcheson	PIL	s	Pilgrim Hymnal
O Holy Spirit Grant Us Grace	Ringvaldt	CON	s	The Lutheran Hymnal
O How I Love Thy Law	James McGranahan	HOP	s	The Service Hymnal
Praise God	Dufford/Foley	NAL	as	A Dwelling Place
Speak, Lord	Tim Schoenbachler	PAA	a	All Is Ready
The Cry Of The Poor	John Foley	NAL	s	Glory And Praise,2
The Heavens Declare Thy Glory	Watts/Mason	HOP	s	Worship & Service Hymnal
The Heavens Declare Thy Glory	Watts/Mason	PIL	s	Pilgrim Hymnal
The Heavens Proclaim	Joseph Gelineau	GIA	s	30 Psalms & 2 Canticles

The Heavens Tell The Glory	S. Somerville	WLP	s	Psalms For Singing,Bk.2
The Law Commands	Isaac Watts	CON	s	The Lutheran Hymnal
The Law Of God Is Good	Matthias Loy	CON	s	The Lutheran Hymnal
The Law Of The Lord	William Callahan	ACP	s	Song Leader's Handbook
The Law Of The Lord	Joseph Gelineau	GIA	s	30 Psalms & 2 Canticles
The Precepts Of The Lord	Kreutz/Gelineau	GIA	st	Gelineau Gradual
The Precepts Of The Lord	E. Diemente	WLP	s	Cantor Book
The Spacious Firmament	Addison/Haydn	PIL	s	Pilgrim Hymnal
The Spacious Firmament	Addison/Haydn	CPF	s	The Hymnal 1940
The Spacious Heavens	Westra/Bourgeois	HOP	s	The Service Hymnal
The Stars Declare His Glory	Dudley-Smith Et Al.	GIA	s	Psalm Praise
Their Message Goes Out	J. G. Phillips	WLP	s	Cantor Book
Their Message Goes Out	Proulx/Gelineau	GIA	s	Gelineau Gradual
Wherever I Am	C. P. Mudd	PAA	a	I Shall See
Your Word, O Lord	C. B. Garve	AUG	s	Lutheran Book Of Worship
Your Words, O Lord	Lucien Deiss	WLP	s	Biblical Hymns & Psalms,2
Your Words, O Lord	Carroll/Gelineau	GIA	st	Gelineau Gradual

20 _____

In The Day Of Need	Idle/Warren	GIA	s	Psalm Praise
May The Lord Answer	Joseph Gelineau	GIA	s	Grail-Gelineau Psalter
Rejoice Ye Pure In Heart	Plumtre/Messiter	MPH	s	The Book Of Hymns
Rejoice O Pilgrim Throng	Plumtre/Messiter	AUG	s	Lutheran Book Of Worship

21 _____

| O Lord, Your Strength Gives | Joseph Gelineau | GIA | s | Grail-Gelineau Psalter |

22

Psalm 22	Theophane Hytrek	GIA	o	
All Who See Me	William Callahan	ACP	s	Song Leader's Handbook
Alleluia (3x)	Douglas Mews	GIA	s	ICEL Lectionary Music
Come Save Me Lord		ACP	s	The Johannine Hymnal
I Will Fulfill	William Callahan	ACP	s	Song Leader's Handbook
I Will Praise You Lord	Angelo Della Picca	WLP	s	CANTOR Book
I Will Praise You Lord	P. Cunningham	PAS	st	Cast Into The Deep
I Will Praise You Lord	Schiavone/Gelineau	GIA	st	Gelineau Gradual
My God, O My God	Carol Dick	PAA	a	Remember Who We Are
My God, My God	Marty Haugen	GIA	s	Psalms For The Church Year
My God, My God	Angelo Della Picca	WLP	s	
My God, My God	C. A. Peloquin	GIA	ao	Songs Of Israel
My God, My God	Christopher Willcock	PAA	ot	Psalms For Feasts & Seasons
My God, My God	David C. Isele	GIA	as	Songs Of David
My God, My God	Howard Hughes	GIA	o	
My God, My God	Joseph Gelineau	GIA	s	30 Psalms & 2 Canticles
My God, My God	P. Cunningham	GRA	ht	
My God, My God	Patti Kostos	FEL		
My God, My God	Schiavone/Gelineau	GIA	st	Gelineau Gradual
My God, My God	W. A. Jurgens	OSB	s	Book Of Sacred Song
My God	Donald J. Reagan	WLP	s	People's Mass Book, 1984
My God, My God	Jerry R. Brubaker			Psalms For The Cantor,1
O God, My God	Robert Twynham	PAA	os	Psalms & Acclamations
O Lord Our Father	Heerman	CON	s	The Lutheran Hymnal
O Lord, Be Not Far	Gregory Norbet	WES	ast	Wherever You Go
O Lord, You've Gone From Me	Jeffrey Hamm	PAA	a	Works Of God
Remember, O Lord	Douglas Mews	IA	s	ICEL Lectionary Music
Song Of Suffering	Jack Miffleton	WLP	ast	Drylands
The Road To Jerusalem	Rory Cooney	NAL	ast	You Alone
Why Have You Abandoned Me?	Rory Cooney	NAL	ast	You Alone

23

Psalm 23	Grayson W. Brown	NAL	o	
Psalm 23	Jack Beeson	OXF	s	The Bay Psalm Book
Psalm 23	R. Vaughan Williams	OXF	o	
Psalm 23	Theophane Hytrek	GIA	o	
Psalm 23	Thom Mason	GIA	o	
A Banquet Is Prepared	John Kavanaugh	NAL	as	Neither Silver Nor Gold
A Banquet Is Prepared	John Kavanaugh	NAL	s	Glory And Praise,2
All My Days	Steven Farney	RPB	amt	Modern Liturgy,12.7
And I Will Follow	Ray Repp	FEL	s	Hymnal For Young Christians
Christ Is Our Leader		ACP	s	The Johannine Hymnal
He Leadeth Me	Gilmore/Bradbury	AUG	s	Lutheran Book Of Worship
He Leadeth Me	Gilmore/Bradbury	MPH	s	The Book Of Hymns
I Am The Good Shepherd	Gerhard Cartford	AUG	o	
I Am The Good Shepherd	M. Shepherd/Cartford	AUG	s	Seasonal Psalms
I Shall Live In The House	Batastini/Gelineau	GIA	st	Gelineau Gradual
I Shall Live In The House	R. J. Schaffer	WLP	s	Cantor Book
I Shall Live In The House	Robert Twynham	PAA	os	Psalms & Acclamations
I Will Dwell In The House	V. Eville	BOH		
In Heavenly Love Abiding	Anna Waring	MPH	s	The Book Of Hymns
Jesus Thy Boundless Love	Gerhard/Cocker	AUG	s	Lutheran Book Of Worship
Like A Shepherd	Bob Dufford	NAL	as	A Dwelling Place
My Shepherd Is The Lord	Robert M. Hutmacher	GIA	o	Choral Series,1985
My Shepherd Is The Lord	F. Hillebrand	AHC	ast	Long Way Home
My Shepherd Is The Lord	Joseph Gelineau	GIA	s	24 Psalms & A Canticle
My Shepherd Is The Lord	Suzanne Toolan	RPB	st	Gather 'Round,Too
O Christe Domine Jesu	Jacques Berthier	GIA	as	Music From Taize,2
Peace I Leave With You	P. Cunningham	GRA	ht	
Shepherd, Lead Me	Dick Hilliard	RPB	ast	My Heart Is Happy
The Living God My Shepherd Is	Driscoll/MacBeth Bain	GIA	s	Worship II
The Lord Is My Shepherd	Montgomery/Koschat	GPH	s	Hymns Of Glorious Praise
The Lord Is My Shepherd	"Crimond"/Irvine	HOP	s	Worship & Service Hymnal
The Lord Is My Shepherd	Angelo Della Picca	WLP	s	Cantor Book
The Lord Is My Shepherd	Dale Wood	GIA	s	ICEL Lectionary Music
The Lord Is My Shepherd	Franz Schubert	OXF		
The Lord Is My Shepherd	Jean Berger	BBL		
The Lord Is My Shepherd	Joe Wise	PAA	ast	Songs For The Journey
The Lord Is My Shepherd	John Foley	NAL	as	Neither Silver Nor Gold
The Lord Is My Shepherd	John M. Talbot	CLM	ast	Come To The Quiet
The Lord Is My Shepherd	Joseph Gelineau	GIA	s	Worship II
The Lord Is My Shepherd	Montgomery/Koschat	HOP	s	Worship & Service Hymnal
The Lord Is My Shepherd	P. Cunningham	GRA	ht	
The Lord Is My Shepherd	Paul Quinlan	FEL	s	Hymnal For Young Christians
The Lord Is My Shepherd	Paul Quinlan	NAL	a	Love And A Question
The Lord Is My Shepherd	Robert Blue	FEL	s	Hymnal For Young Christians
The Lord Is My Shepherd	Robert Twynham	PAA	os	Psalms & Acclamations
The Lord Is My Shepherd	S. Somerville	WLP	s	Psalms For Singing,Bk.1
The Lord Is My Shepherd	Seddon/Warren	GIA	s	Psalm Praise
The Lord Is My Shepherd	St. Columba	AUG	s	Psalms For The Church Year
The Lord Is My Shepherd	Westendorf/Vermulst	WLP	s	People's Mass Book
The Lord Is My Shepherd	Westendorf/Vermulst	WLP	s	People's Mass Book,1984
The Lord Is My Shepherd	William Callahan	ACP	s	Song Leader's Handbook
The Lord Is My Shepherd	Joseph Gelineau	MPH	s	Suppl.To Book Of Hymns
The Lord Is My True Shepherd	Lindusky/Mohr	WLP	s	People's Mass Book,1984
The Lord Is My True Shepherd	Westendorf/Woollen	WLP	s	People's Mass Book
The Lord Is My True Shepherd	Westendorf/Woollen	WLP	s	People's Mass Book,1984
The Lord Is My True Shepherd	E. Lindusky/J.Mohr	WLP	s	People's Mass Book
The Lord My Pasture Shall Prepare	Addison/Carey	CON	s	The Lutheran Hymnal
The Lord My Shepherd Is	Watts/J. S. Bach	CON	s	The Lutheran Hymnal
The Lord Prepares A Banquet	Rory Cooney	NAL	ast	You Alone

The Lord To Me A Shepherd Is	Judy Hunnicut	GIA	o	
The Lord To Me A Shepherd Is	Jean Berger	FLA	o	The Bay Psalm Book
The Lord's My Shepherd	Scottish/J. S. Irvine	GPH	s	Hymns Of Glorious Praise
The Lord's My Shepherd	MacBeth Bain	AUG	s	Lutheran Book Of Worship
The Lord's My Shepherd	Michael Lynch	RAV		
The Lord's My Shepherd	Rous/Gardiner	CON	s	The Lutheran Hymnal
The Lord's My Shepherd	Wyatt	PRO	o	
The Lord's My Shepherd		MPH	s	The Book Of Hymns
The King Of Love	H. W. Baker/Trad. Irish	HEL	s	The Catholic Liturgy Book
The King Of Love	M. Williamson	BOH		
The King Of Love My Shepherd	H. W. Baker	AUG	s	Lutheran Book Of Worship
The King Of Love My Shepherd	Baker/Dykes	CPF	s	The Hymnal 1940
The King Of Love My Shepherd Is	Henry W. Baker	GIA	s	Worship II
Though I Walk In The Valley	Robert Twynham	PAA	os	Psalms & Acclamations
Valleys Of Green	Dan Schutte	NAL	as	Neither Silver Nor Gold
Valleys Of Green	Dan Schutte	NAL	s	Glory And Praise,2
You Have Prepared A Banquet	C. Knoll/F. V. Strahan	HEL	s	The Catholic Liturgy Book

24

All Glory, Laud And Honor	Theodulph Of Orleans	AUG	s	Lutheran Book Of Worship
Fling Wide The Door	Weissel/Freylinghaus	AUG	s	Lutheran Book Of Worship
Glory, Hosanna		ACP	s	The Johannine Hymnal
God Is In His Holy Place	C. A. Peloquin	GIA	o	
Heavens Pour Down Your Waters	C. DeVinck/G. Norbet	WES	ast	Winter's Coming Home
I Have Loved You	Michael Joncas	NAL	ast	On Eagle's Wings
I Have Loved You	Michael Joncas	NAL	s	Glory And Praise,2
Let The Lord Enter	Everett Frese	NPM	s	Advent Psalms
Let The Lord Enter	H. H. Smith	WLP	s	Cantor Book
Let The Lord Enter	Proulx/Gelineau	GIA	st	Gelineau Gradual
Let The King Of Glory Come	Michael Joncas	NAL	ast	On Eagle's Wings
Lift Up Your Heads	John Amner	OXF	o	
Lift Up Your Heads	Orlando Gibbons	OXF	o	
Lift Up Your Heads	Ronald Nelson	AUG	o	
Lift Up Your Heads	Weissel, Winkworth	CON	s	The Lutheran Hymnal
Lift Up Your Heads	Weissel	CPF	s	The Hymnal 1940
Lift Up Your Heads	Winkworth/Williams	MPH	s	The Book Of Hymns
Lift Up Your Heads	Winkworth/Williams	PIL	s	Pilgrim Hymnal
Lift Up Your Heads	Weissel, tr. Winkworth	HEL	s	The Catholic Liturgy Book
Lord This Is The People	Carrol/Gelineau	GIA	st	Gelineau Gradual
Lord This Is The People	Joni Byrne	EKK	at	In Your Presence
Lord This Is The People	Joni Byrne	RPB	m	Modern Liturgy,8.4
Lord This Is The People	Angelo Della Picca	WLP	s	Cantor Book
O God Of God O Light Of Light	John Julian	AUG	s	Lutheran Book Of Worship
Open Wide The Gates	Michael Gilligan	ACP	s	The Johannine Hymnal
Praise The Holy Of Holies	Paul Quinlan	WLP	a	Glory Bound
Prepare The Royal Highway	F. M. Franzen	AUG	s	Lutheran Book Of Worship
The Earth Is The Lord's	Michael Baughen	GIA	s	Psalm Praise
The King Of Glory Comes	Willard F. Jabusch	MPH	s	Suppl. To Book Of Hymns
The Lord's Are The Earth	William Callahan	ACP	s	Song Leader's Handbook
The Lord's Is The Earth	Joseph Gelineau	GIA	s	24 Psalms & A Canticle
The One Whose Deeds	Howard Hughes	GIA	s	Praise God In Song
The Whole Earth Is The Lord's	M. Shepherd/W. Held	AUG	s	Seasonal Psalms
The Whole Earth Is The Lord's	Wilbur Held	AUG	o	
They Shall Receive A Blessing	James Hendrix	ABI	s	Songs Of Zion
This Is The People	Shawn Tracy	PAA	a	He Shall Be Peace
This Is The People	Jeffrey Keyes	RPB	mt	Modern Liturgy,7.2
Who Is This King	H. H. Smith	WLP	s	Cantor Book
Who Is This King	Batastini/Gelineau	GIA	st	Gelineau Gradual
Yahweh, Who Can Enter	Helen Marie Gilsdorf	RPB	m	Modern Liturgy,8.6
Yahweh, Who Can Enter	Helen Marie Gilsdorf	RPB	at	In The Breaking Of Bread

25

Psalm 25	Joseph Gelineau	GIA s	20 Psalms & 3 Canticles
Call To Remembrance	John Hilton	OXF o	
Come O Lord	W. A. Jurgens	OSB s	Book Of Sacred Song
Deliver Us, O God Of Israel	John Foley	NAL as	Neither Silver Nor Gold
Heed My Call For Help	John Foley	NAL as	
Hold Me In Life	Oosterhuis/Huijbers	OCP c	Choral Praise
I Lift My Soul	R. J. Wojcik	ACP s	The Johannine Hymnal
I Lift Up My Soul	Eugene Englert	AUG o	
I Reach Out For You Lord	Jack Miffleton	WLP ast	Drylands
Look Toward Me	John Foley	NAL as	Neither Silver Nor Gold
Look Toward Me	Paul Lisicky	RPB st	Gather 'Round,Too
Miserere Mei	Jacques Berthier	GIA as	Music From Taize,1
O Christe Domine Jesu	Jacques Berthier	GIA as	Music From Taize,2
O God Of Love	Henry W.Baker	AUG s	Lutheran Book Of Worship
Remember Your Mercies	P. Cunningham	GRA ht	
Remember Your Mercies, O Lord	Kreutz/Gelineau	GIA st	Gelineau Gradual
Remember Your Mercies, O Lord	R. J. Schaffer	WLP s	Cantor Book
Remember Your Mercies, O Lord	Wilbur Held	GIA s	ICEL Lectionary Music
Teach Me Your Ways	Michael Lynch	RAV as	There's A Time
Teach Me Your Ways O Lord	Robert Kreutz	WLP s	Cantor Book
Teach Me Your Ways O Lord	Proulx/Gelineau	GIA st	Gelineau Gradual
The Sorrows Of My Heart	William Boyce	OXF o	
Thy Way Not Mine	H. Bonar	CON s	The Lutheran Hymnal
To You I Lift My Soul	S. Somerville	WLP s	Psalms For Singing,Bk.1
To You O Lord	Christopher Willcock	PAA ot	Psalms For Feasts & Seasons
To You O Lord	Marty Haugen	GIA s	Psalms For The Church Year
To You, O Lord	G. Farrell	OSB s	Book Of Sacred Song
To You, O Lord	Thompson/Gelineau	GIA st	Gelineau Gradual
To You, O Lord	C. A. Peloquin	GIA ao	Songs Of Israel
To You, O Lord	Marty Haugen	GIA ast	Gather Us In
To You, O Lord	Michael Joncas	COO	
To You O Lord I Lift My Soul	Robert Kreutz	GIA o	
To You, O Lord,I Lift My Soul	Everett Frese	NPM s	Advent Psalms
To You, O Lord,I Lift My Soul	Wilbur Held	GIA s	ICEL Lectionary Music
Turn To Me, Lord	Wilbur Held	GIA s	ICEL Lectionary Music
Uphold Me In Life	Oosterhuis/Huijbers	NAL as	When From Our Exile
Your Ways O Lord	William Callahan	ACP s	Song Leader's Handbook
Your Ways O Lord	J. M. Burns	WLP s	Cantor Book
Your Ways, O Lord	Carroll/Gelineau	GIA st	Gelineau Gradual

26

Do Justice For Me, Lord	S. Somerville	WLP s	Psalms For Singing,Bk.1
Give Judgment For Me, O Lord	Joseph Gelineau	GIA s	Grail-Gelineau Psalter
I Lift Up My Soul	Tim Manion	NAL st	Glory And Praise,1
I Lift Up My Soul	Tim Manion	NAL as	A Dwelling Place
There Is One Thing I Ask	Tobias Colgan	ABB ast	Songs Like Incense
We Praise Thee, O God	J. B. Cady Cory	CON s	The Lutheran Hymnal
We Praise You O God	Cory/Valerius	AUG s	Lutheran Book Of Worship

27

Psalm 27	Paul Wrynn	PAA as	He Shall Be Peace
Be Strong	Roger Sherman	GIA o	
Christ-light	Robert Blue	FEL s	Hymnal For Young Christians
Do Not Be Afraid	Christopher Willcock	PAA st	Let All The Peoples
God Is My Strong Salvation	James Montgomery	MPH s	The Book Of Hymns
God Is My Strong Salvation	Montgomery/Vulpius	PIL s	Pilgrim Hymnal
I Believe That I Shall See	Michael Lynch	RAV	
I Believe That I Shall See	Robert Kreutz	WLP s	Cantor Book
I Believe That I Shall See	Kelly/Gelineau	GIA st	Gelineau Gradual
I Believe That I Shall See	C. P. Mudd	PAA a	I Shall See
I Believe That I Shall See	Paul Wrynn	PAA a	He Shall Be Peace
I Will Offer Sacrifice	P. Cunningham	GRA h	
Long Live The Lord	Lucien Deiss	WLP s	People's Mass Book
Lord We Come Before Thee	Hammond/Knecht	CON s	The Lutheran Hymnal
My Light And Salvation	P. Cunningham	GRA ht	
Remember Your Love	Balhoff/Ducote Et Al.	NAL s	Glory And Praise,2
Remember Your Love	Balhoff/Ducote Et Al.	NAL ast	Remember Your Love
Safe In The Hands Of God	Perry/Warren	GIA s	Psalm Praise
The Lord Is My Light	Peter Hallock	GIA o	St. Mark's Cathedral Series
The Lord Is My Light	David Haas	GIA s	Psalms for the Church Year
The Lord Is My Light	James M. Burns	WLP s	Psalms for the Cantor,1
The Lord Is My Light	Jacques Berthier	GIA as	Music From Taize,2
The Lord Is My Light	William Callahan	ACP s	Song Leader's Handbook
The Lord Is My Light	E. Englert	GIA o	
The Lord Is My Light	Joseph Gelineau	GIA s	30 Psalms & 2 Canticles
The Lord Is My Light	J. M. Burns	WLP s	Cantor Book
The Lord Is My Light	Joe Zsigray	NAL as	Arise,Come Sing
The Lord Is My Light	J. Coller	OSB s	Book Of Sacred Song
The Lord Is My Light	Pauline Mills	ASA s	Songs Of Praise,1
The Lord Is My Light	Christopher Willcock	PAA ot	Psalms For Feasts & Seasons
The Lord Is My Light	Baughen/Planck	GIA s	Psalm Praise
The Lord Is My Light	John Foley	NAL as	A Dwelling Place
The Lord Is My Light	Arthur Wills	GIA s	ICEL Lectionary Music
The Lord Is My Light	R. Rousseau	RPB mt	Modern Liturgy,5.6
The Lord Is My Light	S. Somerville	WLP s	Psalms For Singing,Bk.2
The Lord Is My Light	Marty Haugen	PAA a	I Send My Light

The Lord Is Near	Michael Joncas	NAL	ast	On Eagle's Wings
This Alone	Tim Manion	NAL	ast	Lord Of Light
We Praise You, O Lord	W. A. Jurgens	OSB	s	Book Of Sacred Song
Whom Shall I Fear	Michael Lynch	RAV	as	There's A Time

28

Grant Us Peace	Michael Gilligan	ACP	s	The Johannine Hymnal
Kyrie, God Father		AUG	s	Lutheran Book Of Worship
Kyrie, God Father In Heaven	Polack, Gustave	CON	s	The Lutheran Hymnal
To You O Lord I Call	Joseph Gelineau	GIA	s	Grail-Gelineau Psalter
Unto Thee Will I Cry	Charles Barnes	OXF	o	

29

Father Almighty	E. J. Wojcik	ACP	s	The Johannine Hymnal
From The Depths	Martin Herbst	ACP	s	The Johannine Hymnal
Give To The Lord	William Callahan	ACP	s	Song Leader's Handbook
Give Tribute To The Lord	S. Somerville	WLP	s	Psalms For Singing,Bk.2
Glory Bound	Paul Quinlan	WLP		
Hear Heaven Thunder	W. Billings	ACP	s	The Johannine Hymnal
May The Lord, Mighty God	Anon/Chin. Folk Tune	MPH	s	Suppl.To Book Of Hymns
O Give The Lord You Sons	Joseph Gelineau	GIA	s	24 Psalms & A Canticle
Remember Your Love	Balhoff/Ducote Et Al.	NAL	as	Remember Your Love
The God Of Heaven Thunders	Perry/Warren	GIA	s	Psalm Praise
The Lord Will Bless	Robert Kreutz	WLP	s	Cantor Book
The Lord Will Bless	Proulx/Gelineau	GIA	st	Gelineau Gradual
You Are A Geat God	Paul F. Page	RPB	mt	Modern Liturgy,5.6

30

Hear, O Lord	John Amner	OXF	o	
I Praise You, O Lord	Mary Grace Zunic	FEL	s	Hymnal For Young Christians
I Will Extol You	William Callahan	ACP	s	Song Leader's Handbook
I Will Praise You Lord	Angelo Della Picca	WLP	s	Cantor Book
I Worship You O God	Seddon/Warren	GIA	s	Psalm Praise
O Lord, Have Mercy	Owen Alstott	OCP	s	Choral Praise — 1985
Oh Sing My Soul	Krohn/Egenolf	AUG	s	Lutheran Book Of Worship
We Are All Held In His Hand	Paul Quinlan	WLP	a	Glory Bound
You Drew Me Clear	Michael Lynch	RAV		
You Have Rescued Me	Dean Olawski	WRD	s	Give Thanks To The Lord

31

Father, I Put My Life	Angelo Della Picca	WLP	s	Cantor Book
Father, I Put My Life	Howard Hughes	GIA	o	
Father, I Put My Life	McKeon/Gelineau	GIA	st	Gelineau Gradual
Have Mercy Upon Me, O Lord	Robert Starer	SOM		
I Put My Life In Your Hands	Marty Haugen	GIA	s	Psalms For The Church Year
In Manibus Tuis	P. Cunningham	GRA	ht	
In Thee Lord	Reusner	CON	s	The Lutheran Hymnal
Into Your Hands	Lucien Deiss	WLP	s	Sing For The Lord
Into Your Hands	Lucien Deiss	WLP	at	Let The Earth Shout
In You O Lord	William Callahan	ACP	s	Song Leader's Handbook
In You O Lord I Take Refuge	Joseph Gelineau	GIA	st	Gelineau Gradual
Jesus Still Lead On	Zingendorf/Drese	AUG	s	Lutheran Book Of Worship
Lord, Be My Rock	Kelly/Gelineau	GIA	st	Gelineau Gradual
Lord, Be My Rock	R. J. Schagger	WLP	s	Cantor Book
My Spirit On Thy Care	Lyte/J. S. Bach	CON	s	The Lutheran Hymnal
Song Of Abandonment	Carey Landry	NAL	a	By Name I Have Called You
The Lord Is Near	Christopher Willcock	GIA	s	ICEL Lectionary Music

32

Psalm 32	Schutz/Reuning	GIA	s	The Becker Psalter
Blest Is The Man	Isaac Watts	CON	s	The Lutheran Hymnal
Happy Is He	William Callahan	ACP	s	Song Leader's Handbook
Happy Is He Whose Offence	Idle/Wilson	GIA	s	Psalm Praise
Happy The Man	Joseph Gelineau	GIA	s	30 Psalms & 2 Canticles
Happy The People	Tobias Colgan	ABB	ast	Songs Like Incense
I Turn To You Lord	Jeffrey Keyes	RPB	mt	Modern Liturgy,7.2
I Turn To You Lord	Carroll/Gelineau	GIA	st	Gelineau Gradual
I Turn To You Lord	J. M. Burns	WLP	s	Cantor Book
Lord Forgive The Wrong	Carroll/Gelineau	GIA	st	Gelineau Gradual
Lord Forgive The Wrong	Robert Kreutz	WLP	s	Cantor Book
Lord When We Bend Before	Carlyle/Day	CON	s	The Lutheran Hymnal
May Your Love Be Upon Us	Tobias Colgan	ABB	ast	Songs Like Incense

33

Psalm 33	Theophane Hytrek	GIA	o	
A Choral Flourish	R. Vaughan Williams	OXF	o	
Blessed Is The Nation	John F. Wilson	HOP	s	Songbk For Saints & Sinners
Cry Out For Joy In The Lord	S. Somerville	WLP	s	Psalms For Singing,Bk.2
Exult You Just	William Callahan	ACP	s	Song Leader's Handbook
Happy The People	Angelo Della Picca	WLP	s	Cantor Book
Happy The People	Kelly/Gelineau	GIA	s	Gelineau Gradual
Lord Let Your Mercy	Carroll/Gelineau	GIA	st	Gelineau Gradual
Lord Let Your Mercy	J. G. Phillips	WLP	s	Cantor Book
Make Music To My God	R. M. Hutmacher	GIA	o	
O God Our Help In Ages Past	Watts/Croft	AUG	s	Lutheran Book Of Worship
Praise God For Everything	Angela Murphy	RPB	st	Gather 'Round, Too
Praise The Lord Ye Just Men	Ludovico Viadana	GIA	o	
Rejoice, Rejoice You Men	Saward/Jacob	GIA	s	Psalm Praise
Ring Out Your Joy	Joseph Gelineau	GIA	s	30 Psalms & 2 Canticles
Ring Out Your Joy To The Lord	Joseph Gelineau	GIA	s	Worship II
The Earth Is Full	Carroll/Gelineau	GIA	st	Gelineau Gradual
The Lord Is Kind And Merciful	Douglas Mews	GIA	s	ICEL Lectionary Music
The Radiance Of His Glory	Suzanne Toolan	RPB	ast	Keeping Festival
This Poor Man Called	Tobias Colgan	ABB	ast	Songs Like Incense
Upright Is The Word	William Callahan	ACP	s	Song Leader's Handbook
When All Thy Mercies	Addison/Este	CON	s	The Lutheran Hymnal
When All Your Mercies	Addison/Kirbye	AUG	s	Lutheran Book Of Worship

34

At All Times I Will Bless	P. Cunningham	GRA	ht	
At All Times I Will Bless	S. Somerville	WLP	s	Psalms For Singing,Bk.1
Come To Him	Russell Woollen	GIA	s	ICEL Lectionary Music
Come, My Children	Balhoff/Daigle Et Al.	NAL	as	Path Of Life
Draw Near And Take The Body	Neale/Sullivan	AUG	s	Lutheran Book Of Worship
Draw Nigh And Take	J. M. Neale	CON	s	The Lutheran Hymnal
Glorify The Lord With Me	Lucien Deiss	WLP	s	People's Mass Book
Glorify The Lord With Me	Lucien Deiss	WLP	s	People's Mass Book,1984
Glory In The Land	James Marchionda	WLP	a	Canticle
I Looked To God	Paul Quinlan	FEL	s	Hymnal For Young Christians
I Will Bless The Lord	Theophane Hytrek	WLP	s	Psalms For The Cantor,1
I Will Bless The Lord	C. Hetherington	GIA	s	Psalm Praise
I Will Bless The Lord	Gerhard Track	OSB	s	Book Of Sacred Song
I Will Bless The Lord	Joseph Gelineau	GIA	s	30 Psalms & 2 Canticles
I Will Bless The Lord	Paul F. Page	RPB	at	Look For The Savior
I Will Bless The Lord	Paul F. Page	RPB	m	Modern Liturgy,7.8
I Will Bless The Lord	Paul Lisicky	RPB	mt	Modern Liturgy,5.7
I Will Bless The Lord	William Callahan	ACP	s	Song Leader's Handbook
O Christe Domine Jesu	Jacques Berthier	GIA	as	Music From Taize,2
O Bless The Lord My Soul	Joe Zsigray	NAL	as	O Bless The Lord My Soul
O Taste And See	R. Vaughan Williams	OXF	o	
O Taste And See	S. Somerville	WLP	s	People's Mass Book,1984
Our Blessing Cup	Michael Joncas	NAL	ast	On Eagle's Wings
Our Blessing Cup	Michael Joncas	NAL	s	Glory And Praise,2
Sanctus Dominus	Jacques Berthier	GIA	as	Music From Taize,2
Sing To The Lord	Ken Medema	WRD	s	Pilgrim Praise
Son Of David	John Foley	NAL	s	Glory And Praise,2
Taste And See	Randolph Currie	GIA	o	Choral Series G2824
Taste And See	Marty Haugen	GIA	s	Psalms For The Church Year
Taste And See	Angelo Della Picca	WLP	o	
Taste And See	C. A. Peloquin	GIA	ao	Songs Of Israel
Taste And See	Christopher Willcock	PAA	ot	Psalms For Feasts & Seasons
Taste And See	Howard Hughes	RPB	st	Gather 'Round, Too
Taste And See	Marty Haugen	PAA	ast	With Open Hands
Taste And See	P. Cunningham	GRA	st	Cast Into The Deep
Taste And See	Patrick Cunningham	RPB	st	Gather 'Round, Too
Taste And See	Proulx/Gelineau	GIA	st	Gelineau Gradual
Taste And See	Ron Ellis	RAV	as	There's A Time
Taste And See	Russell Woollen	GIA	s	ICEL Lectionary Music
Taste And See	Tim Schoenbachler	PAA	ast	All Is Ready
The Lord Hears The Cry	J. G. Phillips	WLP	s	Cantor Book
The Lord Hears The Cry	Proulx/Gelineau	GIA	st	Gelineau Gradual
The Lord Is Kind And Merciful	Gerhard Track	OSB	s	Book Of Sacred Song
The Lord Is Kind	J. Coller	OSB	s	Book Of Sacred Song
The Angel Of The Lord	Angelo Della Picca	WLP	s	Cantor Book
The Angel Of The Lord	Proulx/Gelineau	GIA	st	Gelineau Gradual
The Cry Of The Poor	John Foley	NAL	as	Wood Hath Hope
The Cry Of The Poor	John Foley	NAL	s	Glory And Praise,2
Through All The Changing	G. T. Smart	PIL	s	Pilgrim Hymnal
Through All The Changing	Tate, Brady	CON	s	The Lutheran Hymnal
Through All The Changing	Tate, Brady/Lampe	MPH	s	The Book Of Hymns

35

| O Lord, Plead My Cause | Joseph Gelineau | GIA | s | Grail-Gelineau Psalter |
| The Earth Is Full | Joe Zsigray | NAL | as | Sing A Song Of Love |

36

Awake My Soul	Medley/Herman	CON	s	The Lutheran Hymnal
High In The Heavens	Watts/Williams	PIL	s	Pilgrim Hymnal
How Great And Good Is He	J. S. Bach	ACP	s	The Johannine Hymnal
How Precious	Randall DeBruyn	OCP	s	Choral Praise — 1985
How Precious	Samuel Adler	OXF	o	
Sin Speaks To The Sinner	Joseph Gelineau	GIA	s	Grail-Gelineau Psalter

37

Babylon	Tim Schoenbachler	PAA	a	All Is Ready
Ballad Of The Exiles	Carol Dick	PAA	a	Remember Who We Are
Commit Whatever Grieves Thee	Gerhardt/Hassler	CON	s	The Lutheran Hymnal
Do Not Fret	Joseph Gelineau	GIA	s	Grail-Gelineau Psalter
Give To The Winds Thy Fear	Wesley/Howard	MPH	s	The Book Of Hymns
When Lawless Men Succeed	Idle/Warren	GIA	s	Psalm Praise

38

Psalm 38	Schutz/Reuning	GIA	s	The Becker Psalter
Alas My God My Sins Are Great	Major, Winkworth	CON	s	The Lutheran Hymnal
O God Forsake Me Not	Frank, Crull	CON	s	The Lutheran Hymnal
O Lord, Do Not Rebuke Me	Joseph Gelineau	GIA	s	Grail-Gelineau Psalter

39

A Pilgrim And A Stranger	Gerhardt/Hassler	CON	s	The Lutheran Hymnal
I Said "I Will Be Watchful"	Joseph Gelineau	GIA	s	Grail-Gelineau Psalter
Lord Let Me Know Mine End	Maurice Greene	OXF	o	
When My Heart Was Burning Up	Paul Quinlan	FEL	s	Hymnal For Young Christians

40

Psalm 40	Samuel Adler	OXF	o	
Happy Are They	Steven Farney	RPB	amt	Modern Liturgy,12.7
Here I Am, O Lord	Michael Lynch	RAV		
Here Am I, Lord	H. H. Smith	WLP	s	Cantor Book
Here Am I, Lord	Proulx/Gelineau	GIA	st	Gelineau Gradual
Here Am I, Lord	Donald J. Reagan	WLP	s	People's Mass Book,1984
I Have Waited	Helen Marie Gilsdorf	RPB	m	Modern Liturgy,8.5
I Have Waited	William Callahan	ACP	s	Song Leader's Handbook
I Have Waited	Helen Marie Gilsdorf	RPB	at	In The Breaking Of Bread
I Have Waited For The Lord	P. Cunningham	GRA	ht	
I Waited For The Lord	Joseph Gelineau	GIA	s	20 Psalms & 3 Canticles
I Waited Patiently	Michael Baughen	GIA	s	Psalm Praise
In Your Presence	Joni Byrne	RPB	m	Modern Liturgy,8.3
In Your Presence	Joni Byrne	EKK	as	In Your Presence
Lord As Thou Wilt	Bienmann	CON	s	The Lutheran Hymnal
Lord Come To My Aid	Batastini/Gelineau	GIA	st	Gelineau Gradual
Lord Come To My Aid	Angelo Della Picca	WLP	s	Cantor Book
Praise Alleluia!	H. Lyte/B. Burroughs	FLA	o	
The Lord Hath Put A New Song	M. Armstrong Farra	ERD	s	Sound Of Living Waters
The Lord Put A New Song	Anthony Lawrence	RPB	mt	Modern Liturgy,4.8
Wake Up, My Soul	Hal H. Hopson	CFS	o	

41

Happy Is He	William Callahan	ACP	s	Song Leader's Handbook
Happy Is He Who Regards	P. Cunningham	GRA	ht	
Lord Heal My Soul	Carroll/Gelineau	GIA	st	Gelineau Gradual
Lord Heal My Soul	Robert Kreutz	WLP	s	Cantor Book
May God Be Praised	Jackie Schmitz	RPB	st	Gather 'Round,Too

42

And By Night A Song	Richard J. Meyette	RPB	mt	Modern Liturgy,11.5
As A Doe	Mike Fitzgerald	ERD	s	Sound Of Living Waters
As A Doe	Mike Fitzgerald	WGM	as	Songs Of Praise,2
As A Doe	Bob Rowe	WLP	s	People's Mass Book,1984
As Longs The Deer	Tate, Brady/Englert	GIA	o	Choral Series,1985
As Pants The Hart	Tate, Brady/Spohr	CON	s	The Lutheran Hymnal
As Pants The Hart	Tate, Brady/Wilson	CPF	s	The Hymnal 1940
As Pants The Hart	Tate, Brady/Finlay	MPH	s	The Book Of Hymns
As Pants The Hart	H. R. Wilson	PIL	s	Pilgrim Hymnal
As Pants The Hart	Tate, Brady/Wilson	AUG	s	Lutheran Book Of Worship
As The Deer	Charles Culbreth	RPB	at	Conversation
As The Deer	Oosterhuis/Huijbers	NAL	as	When From Our Exile
As The Deer	Charles Culbreth	RPB	mt	Modern Liturgy,7.5
As The Deer Longs	Jeanette Goglia	RPB	m	Modern Liturgy,10.6
As The Deer Longs For Water	Michael Baughen	GIA	s	Psalm Praise
As The Deer Yearns	Westendorf/Picca	WLP	s	People's Mass Book
As The Hart	Danna Harkin	WRD	s	New Heaven, New Earth
As The Hart About To Falter	Westra/Bourgeois	HOP	s	The Service Hymnal
As The Hart Panteth	Gordon Hawkins	OXF	o	
As The Wild Deer	G. P. Palestrina	GIA	o	
Athirst Is My Soul	William Callahan	ACP	s	Song Leader's Handbook
Face To Face	F. Hillebrand	AHC	ast	Long Way Home
Fran's Song	Ken Meltz	WLP	ast	Hundredfold
God Is Our Refuge	Marty Haugen	PAA	a	I Send My Light
Long For You, My God	Carol Dick	COO		
I Thirst For You	Tim Schoenbachler	NAL	ast	O Jerusalem
Jerusalem My Happy Home	Reinagle	CON	s	The Lutheran Hymnal
Judica Me, Deus	G. G. Gorczycki	GIA	o	
Like A Deer In Winter	Paul Quinlan	NAL		
Like A Deer That Longs	J. G. Phillips	WLP	s	Cantor Book
Like A Deer That Yearns	Joseph Gelineau	GIA	s	24 Psalms & A Canticle
Like A Hart	M. Williamson	BOH		
My Soul Thirsts	Rick Bennett	RPB	mt	Modern Liturgy,6.1
My Soul Thirsts For The Lord	Paul Quinlan	WLP		

O Mortal Man		ACP	s	The Johannine Hymnal
Song Of The Exile	Marty Haugen	PAA	ast	With Open Hands
When Can I Enter	C. Knoll/F. V. Strahan	HEL	s	The Catholic Liturgy Book
You Will Draw Water	Tom Conry	NAL	a	We The Living

43

Defend Me O God	Joseph Gelineau	GIA	s	24 Psalms & A Canticle
Defend Me, O God	Joseph Gelineau	GIA	s	Worship II
Face To Face	F. Hillebrand	AHC	ast	Long Way Home
O God Of God, O Light Of Light	John Julian	CON	s	The Lutheran Hymnal
To You I Lift Up My Soul	John Kavanaugh	NAL	as	Neither Silver Nor Gold
Why Art Thou So Heavy My Soul	H. Loosemire	OXF	o	

44

Awake, Do Not Cast Us Off	Samuel Adler	OXF	o	
O Lord Our Fathers	Tate, Brady/Kirbye	MPH	s	The Book Of Hymns
We Heard With Our Own Ears	Joseph Gelineau	GIA	s	Grail-Gelineau Psalter
Your Word Has Cut Us		ACP	s	The Johannine Hymnal

45

As A Lily Among Thorns	Westendorf/Picca	WLP	s	People's Mass Book
Beautiful Savior		AUG	s	Lutheran Book Of Worship
Beautiful Savior		CON	s	The Lutheran Hymnal
Come, Thou Almighty King	Giardini	AUG	s	Lutheran Book Of Worship
For Assumption	P. Cunningham	GRA	ht	
In Your Splendor And Beauty	A. D'Achille	OSB	s	Benedictine Book Of Song
My Heart Overflows	Joseph Gelineau	GIA	s	20 Psalms & 3 Canticles
O Morning Star	Winkworth/Nicolai	MPH	s	The Book Of Hymns
The Queen Stands	Angelo Della Picca	WLP	s	Cantor Book
The Queen Stands	Carroll/Gelineau	GIA	st	Gelineau Gradual
The Queen Stands	Howard Hughes	GIA	o	
What Grace, O Lord	Monsell/Vulpius	MPH	s	The Book Of Hymns

46

A Mighty Fortress Is Our God	Martin Luther	PIL	s	Pilgrim Hymnal
A Mighty Fortress Is Our God	Martin Luther	AUG	s	Lutheran Book Of Worship
A Mighty Fortress Is Our God	Martin Luther	CON	s	The Lutheran Hymnal
A Mighty Fortress Is Our God	Martin Luther	WLP	s	People's Mass Book
Be Still	Angela Murphy	RPB	st	Gather 'Round, Too
Be Still, Jerusalem	James Marchionda	WLP	ast	Covenant
Be Still My Soul	von Schlegel/Sibelius	CON	s	The Lutheran Hymnal
Be Still My Soul	Borthwick/Sibelius	HOP	s	Worship & Service Hymnal
God Is For Us A Refuge	Anders	AUG	o	
God Is For Us A Refuge	Joseph Gelineau	GIA	s	20 Psalms & 3 Canticles
God Is Our Refuge	Roman/Lunn	CFP		
God Is Our Refuge	Martin Luther	HEL	s	The Catholic Liturgy Book
God Is Our Strength	Bewes/Baughen	GIA	s	Psalm Praise
God Of My Life	William Cowper	CON	s	The Lutheran Hymnal
Grant Us Peace	Michael Gilligan	ACP	s	The Johannine Hymnal
Lord, As A Pilgrim	Malmivaara/Nyberg	AUG	s	Lutheran Book Of Worship
Mighty Lord Is With Us	Dale Wood	AUG	o	
O God Of Every Nation	Reid/Wood	AUG	s	Lutheran Book Of Worship
O God Of Love	Henry W. Baker	AUG	s	Lutheran Book Of Worship
The Lord Of Hosts Is With Us	C.Knoll/F.V.Strahan	HEL	s	The Catholic Liturgy Book
The Mighty Lord Is With Us	M.Shepherd/D.Wood	AUG	s	Seasonal Psalms
There Is A River	Rory Cooney	RPB	amt	Modern Liturgy,10.2
There Is A River	Rory Cooney	RPB	at	If I Forget You,Jerusalem

47

Psalm 47	Charles H. Webb	CHO	o	
Psalm 47	Jack Beeson	OXF	s	The Bay Psalm Book
All Nations Clap Your Hands	S. Somerville	WLP	s	Psalms For Singing,Bk.2
All Peoples Clap Your Hands	Joseph Gelineau	GIA		
All You Nations Clap Your Hands	Paul Lisicky	RPB	mt	Modern Liturgy,6.7
All You People Clap Your Hands	Joseph Roff	GIA	o	
All You Peoples	William Callahan	ACP	s	Song Leader's Handbook
Clap Your Hands	Larry Florian	PAA	as	More Than The Sands
Clap Your Hands	Paul Quinlan	FEL	s	Hymnal For Young Christians
God Has Gone Up	M.Shepherd/W.L.Pelz	AUG	s	Seasonal Psalms
God Has Gone Up	Walter Pelz	AUG	o	
God Mounts His Throne	Marty Haugen	GIA	s	Psalms For The Church Year
God Mounts His Throne	David C. Isele	GIA	as	Songs Of David
God Mounts His Throne	Howard Hughes	GIA	o	
God Mounts His Throne	Kreutz/Gelineau	GIA	st	Gelineau Gradual
God Mounts His Throne	P. Cunningham	GRA	ht	
God Mounts His Throne	W. A. Jurgens	OSB	s	Book Of Sacred Song
God Mounts His Throne	C. A. Peloquin	GIA	ao	Songs Of Israel
God Mounts His Throne	Christopher Willcock	PAA	ot	Psalms For Feasts & Seasons
God Mounts His Throne	M. Haugen	GIA	as	Psalms For The Church Year
Lo, God To Heaven Ascendeth	Sacer, Cox	CON	s	The Lutheran Hymnal
O Clap Your Hands	Hilary Newsom	GIA	s	Psalm Praise
O Clap Your Hands	John Rutter	OXF	o	
O Clap Your Hands	Orlando Gibbons	OXF	o	
O Clap Your Hands	Robert Powell	GIA		
O Clap Your Hands	Gordon Young	OXF	o	
Praise The Lord Ye Lands	Westra/Bourgeois	HOP	s	The Service Hymnal
Shout To God With Gladness	Angel Tucciarone	WLP	s	Hundredfold
Sing Halleluia Praise The Lord	Paul Quinlan	FEL	s	Hymnal For Young Christians
Sing To The Lord	Ken Medema	WRD	s	Pilgrim Praise
Sing To The Lord	Han Van Koert	ACP	s	The Johannine Hymnal

48

Come Where The Wind Is Free		ACP	s	The Johannine Hymnal
Great Is The Lord	Idle/Warren	GIA	s	Psalm Praise
Great Is The Lord	Isaac Watts	CON	s	The Lutheran Hymnal
How Great And Good Is He	J. S. Bach	ACP	s	The Johannine Hymnal
How Great Is God	Bewes/Wilson	GIA	s	Psalm Praise
Salem City		ACP	s	The Johannine Hymnal
The Lord Is Great	Joseph Gelineau	GIA	s	Grail-Gelineau Psalter
We Wait For Thy Loving	William McKie	OXF	o	
We Wait For Thy Loving	Stephen Elvey	OXF	o	

49

Hear This All You Peoples	Joseph Gelineau	GIA	s	Grail-Gelineau Psalter

50

Psalm 50	F. M. Christiansen	AUG	o	
From Sion Perfect In Beauty	Robert Kreutz	GIA	o	
God The Lord	William Callahan	ACP	s	Song Leader's Handbook
How Can I Thank Thee	Denicke	CON	s	The Lutheran Hymnal
To The Upright I Will Show	Batastini/Gelineau	GIA	st	Gelineau Gradual
To The Upright I Will Show	E. Diemente	WLP	s	Cantor Book
To The Upright I Will Show	P. Cunningham	GRA	ht	
Turn To Me, Lord	Tim Schoenbachler	NAL	ast	O Jerusalem

51

Psalm 51	John M. Talbot	CLM	ast	Come To The Quiet
Psalm 51	Schutz/Reuning	GIA	s	The Becker Psalter
A Clean Heart	William Callahan	ACP	s	Song Leader's Handbook
A Humbled, Contrite Heart	C.Knoll/F.V.Strahan	HEL	s	The Catholic Liturgy Book
Be Merciful	Michael Lynch	RAV	as	With All My Heart
Be Merciful O Lord	G. Farrell	OSB	s	Book Of Sacred Song
Be Merciful O Lord	Christopher Willcock	PAA	ot	Psalms For Feasts & Seasons
Be Merciful O Lord	Carroll/Gelineau	GIA	st	Gelineau Gradual
Be Merciful O Lord	David C. Isele	GIA	as	Songs Of David
Be Merciful, O Lord	Douglas Mews	WLP	s	Psalms For The Cantor, 1
Be Merciful, O Lord	Ralph C. Verdi	GIA	s	ICEL Lectionary Music
Be Merciful, O Lord	Douglas Mews	GIA	s	ICEL Lectionary Music
Clean Heart	Ron Ellis	RAV		
Cleanse Me Of Sin O Lord	P. Cunningham	PAS	ot	
Come Holy Spirit Come	Hart/Mason	CON	s	The Lutheran Hymnal
Create A Clean Heart	Schiavone/Gelineau	GIA	st	Gelineau Gradual
Create A Clean Heart	J. M. Burns	WLP	s	Cantor Book
Create A Clean Heart In Me	Ralph C. Verdi	GIA	s	ICEL Lectionary Music
Create In Me	Johannes Brahms			
Create In Me	Marty Haugen	PAA	a	I Send My Light
Father, Mercy	Bob Dufford	NAL	as	Neither Silver Nor Gold
Give Me A Clean Heart	Margaret Douroux	MPH	s	Suppl. To Book Of Hymns
Have Mercy	Nicholas Brady	WLP	s	People's Mass Book, 1984
Have Mercy	A. Gregory Murray	WLP	s	People's Mass Book, 1984
Have Mercy Lord	Barnes/Wilson	GIA	s	Psalm Praise
Have Mercy, Lord	Paul Quinlan	FEL	s	Hymnal For Young Christians
Have Mercy, O God	Westendorf/Takacs	WLP	s	People's Mass Book
Have Mercy On Me	Donald J. Reagan	NPM	s	Mercy, Mercy
Have Mercy On Me	Joseph Gelineau	GIA	s	Worship II
Have Mercy On Me	C. A. Peloquin	GIA	ao	Songs Of Israel
Have Mercy On Me	Joseph Gelineau	GIA	s	24 Psalms & A Canticle
Have Mercy On Me	William Callahan	ACP	s	Song Leader's Handbook
Have Mercy On Me, Lord	S. Somerville	WLP	s	Psalms For Singing,Bk.1
I Will Rise	Angelo Della Picca	WLP	s	Cantor Book
I Will Rise	Carroll/Gelineau	GIA	st	Gelineau Gradual
Lenten Psalm	Jeffrey Keyes	RPB	a	A Gentle Strength
Lenten Psalm	Jeffrey Keyes	RPB	mt	Modern Liturgy, 11.6
Lord, Have Mercy	Anthony Lawrence	RPB	mt	Modern Liturgy,7.1
Lord, Teach Us How To Pray	Montgomery/Gibbons	AUG	s	Lutheran Book Of Worship
Miserere	Gregorio Allegri	NOV	o	
O For A Heart To Praise My God	Charles Wesley	MPH	s	The Book Of Hymns
O Thou That Hear'st	Isaac Watts	CON	s	The Lutheran Hymnal
Remember Your Love	John Lee	OSB	s	Book Of Sacred Song
Savior More Than Life To Me	Crosby/Doane	MPH	s	The Book Of Hymns
The Olive Tree	H. B. Hays	OSB	s	Book Of Sacred Song
The Sacrifice You Accept	Michael Joncas	GIA	s	Praise God In Song
The Sacrifice You Accept	David C. Isele	GIA	s	Praise God In Song
The Sacrifice You Accept	Howard Hughes	GIA	s	Praise God In Song
To You Omniscient Lord	Landstat/Schumann	AUG	s	Lutheran Book Of Worship
Turn Thy Face From My Sins	Matthew Locke	OXF	o	

52

Tree Of Life	Suzanne Toolan	RPB	ast	Keeping Festival
Why Do You Boast?	Joseph Gelineau	GIA	s	Grail-Gelineau Psalter

53

The Fool Has Said	Joseph Gelineau	GIA	s	Grail-Gelineau Psalter

54

Come Lord Bring Us	Tobias Colgan	ABB	ast	Songs Like Incense
O God By Your Name	William Callahan	ACP	s	Song Leader's Handbook
The Lord Upholds My Life	Joseph Gelineau	GIA	st	Gelineau Gradual
The Lord Upholds My Life	E. Diemente	WLP	s	Cantor Book

55

God, Hear Me Calling	Helen Marie Gilsdorf	RPB	st	Gather 'Round, Too
If Thou But Suffer God	Neumark	CON	s	The Lutheran Hymnal
If Thou But Suffer God	Winkworth/Neumark	MPH	s	The Book Of Hymns
If You But Trust In God	Georg Neumark	AUG	s	Lutheran Book Of Worship

Let Me Be Yours Forever | N. Selnecker | AUG | s | Lutheran Book Of Worship
O God Listen To My Prayer | Joseph Gelineau | GIA | s | Grail-Gelineau Psalter
When Streaming From The Earth | William Shrubsole | CON | s | The Lutheran Hymnal

56

Have Mercy On Me | Joseph Gelineau | GIA | s | Grail-Gelineau Psalter
Merciful And Gracious Be | Dudley-Smith/Warren | GIA | s | Psalm Praise
Rejoice My Heart | Gerhardt, Kelly | CON | s | The Lutheran Hymnal

57

All Praise To Thee, My God | Ken/Tallis | AUG | s | Lutheran Book Of Worship
Alleluia | Bob Hurd | FEL | |
Be Gracious To Me Lord | Perry/Warren | GIA | s | Psalm Praise
Exalt Yourself | David Hurd | GIA | o | Choral Series, 1985
Have Mercy On Me | Joseph Gelineau | GIA | s | Grail-Gelineau Psalter
Praise The Lord O My Soul | Chris Aridas | RPB | m | Modern Liturgy,8.8
Praise The Lord O My Soul | Chris Aridas | RPB | at | Like The Dawn

Adaptation of Psalm 55

There are many types of literature in the Scriptures: prose, poetry, song, letters, novels, puns, riddles, diaries. Some of them are designed to appeal to the intellect, as in the history of David's reign, for instance. The prophets appealed to the human conscience. And writings such as the Law Codes and the Wisdom Literature influenced whole groups of people in the way they interacted. But it was the Psalms, the prayer of the Anawim, that appealed to the human heart.

God always seems to have been interested in hearts, even more than in minds and bodies. Perhaps it is because our hearts can grasp something of God's love, even when our bodies are tired and our minds fail utterly in contemplation of the Infinite. When God wanted to tell Israel of his faithful love, he said to the author of Isaiah 40, "Speak tenderly to the heart of Jerusalem." Jesus described himself as being "gentle of heart." The Psalms plumb the very depths of the human heart, where faith and doubt, joy and grief, love and hate, hope and despair meet the struggle for possession of the whole person. Ever since the Psalms were first collected and written down in ancient Israel, they have provided a valuable means by which the heart of humanity could vocalize and shape the inner conflict.

Psalms are the prayers, the hymns, of real people who have real joys and sorrows, not with hypothetical or idealized feelings. The courage of some psalms is immense. Imagine the strength it took to frame Psalm 87, for instance: in it the psalmist muses on a life of grief and failure and ends, not with the ideal ending, hope, but with the thought, "my only friend is darkness." The psalm is brutal, but the feelings, though harsh, are completely honest. The Church has metaphorically put this psalm and the other complaint psalms in the mouth of the suffering Christ.

The honesty of the psalms is reflected in Catherine de Vinck's poem, which is itself a meditation on and a development of Psalm 55. The poem complains, questions and groans over many sorrows and evils, but in the end still has hope. The person behind the poem may be anyone in deep distress. It might be Jesus in Gethsemane. It might be a mother in Africa, wondering if there will be food to keep her family from starvation. In the end, the person behind the poem hopes somehow for a resurrection, a Jesus-resurrection, a Christian-resurrection, a world-resurrection.

Eileen E. Freeman

First published in *Modern Liturgy,* 3.4,

April, 1976

Renew My Spirit

Evening, morning, noon
I complain, I groan.
On axles of bones, the body's machine moves
propelled by the wish to go
from here to—where?
Destiny, destination: the wheel turns.
Eternity pumps blood into the veins
arranges the cosmos pleasantly:
the toy-mountain slopes to the village;
the little white houses have brooms
in the hands of little women: they sweep
time's honored dust
return it to the rising wind.
Cycles are never broken
that send mourners to the streets
ring glad bells over the newly born.

I complain, I groan, make lists of black woes:
ants in the sugar, bugs in the flour
solitude turning to loneliness
sticking to the skin
like a dress impossible to peel.
Of dreams I had my share:
daisy-white and tulip-red, they popped
in the air like tired balloons.
Who sold them to me? Who was the vendor
by the fountain in the park?
Spring returns, yes, to stretch green webs
over old trees, but the poor and the dead
are always with us: they sit on the benches
nodding, flaunting their rags
in April's leafing light.
The bread I chew does not defeat my hunger
and all the fire I own is one blue ring
flame enough to heat a cup of rain.

I complain, I groan, lift
my wooden bowl, my open beggar-palms.
The crumbs on the floor are for mice and crickets.
Am I not more than a sparrow
and in need of more gold
than the proverbial lily?

Give me another day, Lord:
    evening, morning, noon
    tomorrow will be a season
    of daffodils, of beauty
    yellow in the grass.

Catherine de Vinck
©1976 Alleluia Press
Psalm 55

58

| Do You Truly Speak Justice | Joseph Gelineau | GIA | s | Grail-Gelineau Psalter |

59

Almighty Lord Before Thy Throne	Steele/Chetham	CON	s	The Lutheran Hymnal
For Thy Mercy And Thy Grace	H. Downton	CON	s	The Lutheran Hymnal
For Your Sake	William Callahan	ACP	s	Song Leader's Handbook
Judge Eternal	Holland/Kittel	CON	s	The Lutheran Hymnal
Rescue Me, God	Joseph Gelineau	GIA	s	Grail-Gelineau Psalter

60

| O God, You Have Rejected Me | Joseph Gelineau | GIA | s | Grail-Gelineau Psalter |

61

From The End Of The Earth	Alan Hovhaness	CFP	o	
Listen To My Prayer Lord	Seddon/Warren	GIA	s	Psalm Praise
My God Is A Rock	R. J. Wojcik	ACP	s	The Johannine Hymnal
O God Hear My Cry	Joseph Gelineau	GIA	s	20 Psalms & 3 Canticles
O God, Our Help In Ages Past	Watts/Croft	AUG	s	Lutheran Book Of Worship
O Sometimes The Shadows	Johnson/Fischer	MPH	s	The Book Of Hymns

62

Psalm 62	C. P. Mudd	PAA	ast	I Shall See
Psalm 62	John M. Talbot	CLM	ast	Come To The Quiet
In God Alone	F. Andersen	RPB	m	Modern Liturgy,8.2
In Silence My Soul Is Waiting	Saward/Strover	GIA	s	Psalm Praise
My Soul Is At Rest	Jacques Berthier	GIA	as	Music From Taize, 2
Only In God	John Foley	NAL	as	A Dwelling Place
Only In God	William Callahan	ACP		
Only In God	John Foley	NAL	s	Glory And Praise,2
Psalm Of Rest	Joe Raffa	EKK	at	In Your Presence
Psalm Of Rest	Joe Raffa	RPB	m	Modern Liturgy,8.4
Rest In God Alone	J. G. Phillips	WLP	s	Cantor Book
Rest In God Alone	Batastini/Gelineau	GIA	s	Gelineau Gradual
Rest In God Alone My Soul	P. Cunningham	GRA	ht	

63

As Morning Breaks	Michael Joncas	NAL	ast	O Joyful Lord
As Morning Breaks	Howard Hughes	GIA	s	Praise God In Song
As Morning Breaks	John M. Talbot	CLM	ast	Come To The Quiet
As The Watchman	Michael Joncas	COO	ast	Every Stone Shall Cry
Drylands	Jack Miffleton	WLP	ast	Drylands
For You, O Lord	Westendorf/Takass	WLP	s	People's Mass Book
Give The Bread Of Life	Lucien Deiss	WLP	s	People's Mass Book
God You Are My God	Lucien Deiss	WLP	s	Sing For The Lord
God You Are My God	Lucien Deiss	WLP	at	Let The Earth Shout
I Am The Bread Of Life	Eugene E. Englert	WLP	o	Westendorf Series 7938
I Long For You	Balhoff, Daigle Etal	NAL	as	Path Of Life
I Long For You	James Marchionda	WLP	ast	Covenant
I Thirst For You	Tim Schoenbachler	NAL	ast	O Jerusalem
I Will Lift Up My Eyes	Tom Conry	OCP	as	Jesus, Lord
In The Morning I Will Sing	David C. Isele	GIA	s	Praise God In Song
In The Morning I Will Sing	Michael Joncas	GIA	s	Praise God In Song
In The Shadow	Jeanette Goglia	RPB	m	Modern Liturgy,10.6
In The Shadow Of Your Wings	Michael Joncas	GIA	s	Praise God In Song
In The Shadow Of Your Wings	Howard Hughes	GIA	s	Praise God In Song
Land Without Water	F. Hillebrand	AHC	ast	Long Way Home
My Soul Is Thirsting	Dolores M. Hruby	WLP	s	Psalms For The Cantor, 1
My Soul Is Thirsting	Ron Ellis	RAV	as	With All My Heart
My Soul Is Thirsting	Angelo Della Picca	WLP	o	
My Soul Is Thirsting	Christopher Willcock	PAA	ot	Psalms For Feasts & Seasons
My Soul Is Thirsting	G. Farrell	OSB	s	Book Of Sacred Song
My Soul Is Thirsting	N. Niedermeyer	OSB	s	Benedictine Book Of Song
My Soul Is Thirsting	Owen Alstott	MLH		
My Soul Is Thirsting	Proulx/Gelineau	GIA	st	Gelineau Gradual
My Soul Is Thirsting	P. Cunningham	GRA	ht	
O God Eternal	Idle/Traditional	GIA	s	Psalm Praise
O God, You Are My God	William Callahan	ACP	s	Song Leader's Handbook
O God, You Are My God	Joseph Gelineau	GIA	s	30 Psalms & 2 Canticles
O God, You Are My God	A. Gregory Murray	WLP	s	People's Mass Book, 1984
O God, You Are My God	C.Knoll/F.V.Strahan	HEL	s	The Catholic Liturgy Book
Prayer From Ps. 63	Clare F. Sturm	RPB	mt	Modern Liturgy,6.8
Song Of Desire	Greg Tolaas	PAA	as	More Than The Sands
The Lord Is My Light	Peter Hallock	GIA	o	St. Mark's Cathedral Series
You Are The God	Judy O'Sheil	FEL	s	Hymnal For Young Christians
You Are The Lord That I Seek	Jeffrey Keyes	RPB	mt	Modern Liturgy,11.7
Your Love Is Finer Than Life	Marty Haugen	GIA	s	Psalms For The Church Year
Your Love Is Finer Than Life	Marty Haugen	GIA	s	Gather Us In

64

Hear My Voice O God	Joseph Gelineau	GIA	s	Grail-Gelineau Psalter

65

At Thy Feet O God And Father	Burns/Bambridge	MPH	s	The Book Of Hymns
Farmer's Earth Psalm	M. Williamson	BOH		
From 'Come Follow'	Jerry Kramper	GIA		
Glory And Praise To Our God	Dan Schutte	NAL	as	Dwelling Place
Glory And Praise To Our God	Dan Schutte	NAL	st	Glory And Praise,1
God's Joyful Harvest	B. Echols/R.J.Powell	CHO	o	
Great King Of Nations	John H. Gurney	CON	s	The Lutheran Hymnal
O Lord Whose Bounteous Hand		CON	s	The Lutheran Hymnal
Safely Through Another Week	Newton/Ebeling	CON	s	The Lutheran Hymnal
The Earth Is Yours O God	Saward/Dunning	GIA	s	Psalm Praise
The Seed That Falls	Hughes/Gelineau	GIA	st	Gelineau Gradual
The Seed That Falls	Paul Lisicky	RPB	st	Gather 'Round, Too
The Seed That Falls	Robert Kreutz	WLP	s	Cantor Book
Thou O God Art Praised	Joseph Corfe	OXF	o	
Thou Visitest The Earth	Maurice Greene	OXF	o	
To Bless The Earth God Sendeth		MPH	s	The Book Of Hymns
To Thee O Lord Our Hearts	William Dix	MPH	s	The Book Of Hymns
To Thee, O Lord	William Dix	CON	s	The Lutheran Hymnal
To You Our Praise Is Due	Joseph Gelineau	GIA	s	30 Psalms & 2 Canticles
We Praise You, O Lord	Douglas Mews	GIA	s	ICEL Lectionary Music
You Have Visited	William Callahan	ACP	s	Song Leader's Handbook
You Have Visited	P. Cunningham	GRA	ht	

66

Psalm 66	Hamvas	FLA	o	
Psalm 66	Richard Slater	AUG	o	
All The Earth Cry Out	Charles Culbreth	RPB	mt	Modern Liturgy,7.5
All The Earth Cry Out	Charles Culbreth	RPB	at	Conversation
All You Nations	Lucien Deiss	WLP	s	People's Mass Book
All You Nations	Lucien Deiss	WLP	s	People's Mass Book, 1984
Alleluia (3x)	Christopher Willcock	GIA	s	ICEL Lectionary Music
Cry Out To God	Ron Ellis	RAV	as	With All My Heart
Glorious Praise	Dick Hilliard	RPB	mt	Modern Liturgy,5.5
Glory And Praise To Our God	Dan Schutte	NAL	st	Glory And Praise,1
Glory And Praise To Our God	Dan Schutte	NAL	as	A Dwelling Place
Let All The Earth	Marty Haugen	GIA	s	Psalms For The Church Year
Let All The Earth	Carroll/Gelineau	GIA	st	Gelineau Gradual
Let All The Earth	Christopher Willcock	PAA	ot	Psalms For Feasts & Seasons
Let All The Earth	G. Farrell	OSB	s	Book Of Sacred Song
Let All The Earth	Angelo Della Picca	WLP	s	Cantor Book
Let All The Earth	M. Haugen	GIA	as	Psalms For The Church Year
Let All The Earth Cry Out	John H. Olivier	WLP	s	Psalms For The Cantor, 1
Let All The Earth Cry Out	Rory Cooney	NAL	ast	You Alone
Let All The Earth Cry Out	P. Cunningham	GRA	ht	
Let All The Earth Worship	Robert Kreutz	GIA	o	
Let Us Rejoice	Jack Miffleton	WLP	ast	Drylands
Lift Up Your Hearts	Roc O'Connor	NAL	ast	Lord Of Light
Oh, Praise The Lord	J. Fisher/H.L.Hassler	FLA	o	
Prayer From Ps.66	Clare F. Sturm	RPB	mt	Modern Liturgy,6.8
Shout Joyfully	William Callahan	ACP	s	Song Leader's Handbook
Shout Joyfully To God	Mary Grace Zunic	FEL	s	Hymnal For Young Christians
Shout Joyfully To God	Dave Brubeck	SFM	o	Mass — To Hope
Voice Of His Praise	M. Williamson	BOH		
While Yet The Morn	Muhlmann	CON	s	The Lutheran Hymnal
Worship And Praise	Jeffrey Keyes	RPB	mt	Modern Liturgy,5.5

67

Alleluia (3x)	Douglas Mews	GIA	s	ICEL Lectionary Music
Glory Hallelujah	Paul Quinlan	WLP	a	Glory Bound
God Be Merciful Unto Us	Ronald Nelson	MPH	s	The Book Of Hymns
God Of Mercy, God Of Grace	Henry F. Lyte	CON	s	The Lutheran Hymnal
Let The People Praise You	M.Shepherd/D.Wood	AUG	s	Seasonal Psalms
Let The People Praise You	Dale Wood	AUG	o	
Let The Peoples Praise You	M. Balhoff/G. Daigle	NAL	ast	Morning To Night
May God Be Gracious To Us	Hans Leo Hassler	AUG	s	Psalms For The Church Year
May God Be Gracious To Us	Baughen/Tredinnick	GIA	s	Psalm Praise
May God Bestow On Us	Martin Luther	CON	s	The Lutheran Hymnal
May God Bestow On Us	Luther/Greitter	AUG	s	Lutheran Book Of Worship
May God Bless Us	J. M. Burns	WLP	s	Cantor Book
May God Bless Us	Batastini/Gelineau	GIA	st	Gelineau Gradual
May God Have Pity	William Callahan	ACP	s	Song Leader's Handbook
May God Have Pity On Us	Frank Schoen	GIA	o	
May The Peoples Praise You	Helen Marie Gilsdorf	RPB	at	In The Breaking Of Bread
May The Peoples Praise You	Helen Marie Gilsdorf	RPB	m	Modern Liturgy,8.5
Mercy, Blessing, Favour	Dudley-Smith/Wilson	GIA	s	Psalm Praise
Mercy, Blessing, Favour	Dudley-Smith/Davies	GIA	s	Psalm Praise
O God Be Gracious	Joseph Gelineau	GIA	s	30 Psalms & 2 Canticles
O God Be Gracious	C. Knoll/F. V. Strahan	HEL	s	The Catholic Liturgy Book
O God Be Merciful	Christopher Tye	GIA	o	
O God Let All The Nations	Carroll/Gelineau	GIA	st	Gelineau Gradual
O God Let All The Nations	Robert Kreutz	WLP	s	Cantor Book
O God May Your Face	Thornton/Trad.	GIA	s	Psalm Praise
O God, Pity Us	P. Cunningham	GRA	ht	

68

Psalm 68	Bernard Rogers	SOM		
Father Almighty	R. J. Wojcik	ACP	s	The Johannine Hymnal
God In Your Goodness	Batastini/Gelineau	GIA	st	Gelineau Gradual
God In Your Goodness	J. M. Burns	WLP	s	Cantor Book
God In Your Goodness	P. Cunningham	GRA	ht	
Hallelujah!	Paul Quinlan	WLP	a	Glory Bound
Let God Arise	M. Williamson	BOH		
Let God Arise	Peloquin/Gelineau	GIA	st	Gelineau Gradual
Lord In Your Tenderness	Lucien Deiss	WLP	s	Biblical Hymns & Psalms,2
See The Conqueror	Wordsworth/Smart	CON	s	The Lutheran Hymnal
Sing To God O Kingdoms	P. Cunningham	GRA	ht	
Stand Up O God	Saward/Wilson	GIA	s	Psalm Praise
The Just Rejoice	William Callahan	ACP	s	Song Leader's Handbook

69

For The Waters Are Come In	Alan Hovhaness	SOM	o	
Hear Us O Lord	Balhoff/Ducote Et Al	NAL	as	Remember Your Love
I Pray To You	William Callahan	ACP	s	Song Leader's Handbook
Jerusalem My Happy Home	A. M. Buchanan	ACP	s	The Johannine Hymnal
Lord In Your Great Love	J. M. Burns	WLP	s	Cantor Book
Lord In Your Great Love	Peloquin/Gelineau	GIA	st	Gelineau Gradual
Lord In Your Great Love	P. Cunningham	GRA	ht	
Save Me	Paul Quinlan	WLP	a	Glory Bound
The Lord Is Kind And Merciful	Christopher Willcock	GIA	s	ICEL Lectionary Music
Turn To The Lord	Carroll/Gelineau	GIA	st	Gelineau Gradual
Turn To The Lord	Angelo Della Picca	WLP	s	Cantor Book

70

O God Make Haste	Joseph Gelineau	GIA	s	30 Psalms & 2 Canticles

71

I Will Sing Of Your Salvation	Angelo Della Picca	WLP	s	Cantor Book
I Will Sing Of Your Salvation	Carroll/Gelineau	GIA	st	Gelineau Gradual
In You O Lord	William Callahan	ACP	s	Song Leader's Handbook
Lord Come Quickly	Jeffrey Keyes	RPB	mt	Modern Liturgy,7.1
Since My Mother's Womb	Kreutz/Gelineau	GIA	st	Gelineau Gradual
With Words Of Praise	Lucien Deiss	WLP	s	Biblical Hymns & Psalms,2

72

All Hail The Lord's Anointed	J.Montgomery	HEL	s	The Catholic Liturgy Book
Come, O Lord	Douglas Mews	GIA	s	ICEL Lectionary Music
Every Nation On Earth	Marty Haugen	GIA	s	Psalms For The Church Year
Give The King	C. F. Witt	ACP	s	The Johannine Hymnal
Give The King	Matthias Lorenz	ACP	s	The Johannine Hymnal
Glory Hosanna		ACP	s	The Johannine Hymnal
Hail To The Lord's Anointed	Montgomery/Noble	PIL	s	Pilgrim Hymnal
Hail To The Lord's Anointed	Montgomery/Schroter	CON	s	The Lutheran Hymnal
Hail To The Lord's Anointed	J. Montgomery	CPF	s	The Hymnal 1940
He Shall Rule From Sea To Sea	Godfrey Schroth	GIA	o	
Jesus Shall Reign	Watts/Hatton	GPH	s	Hymns Of Glorious Praise
Jesus Shall Reign	Watts/Hatton	HOP	s	Worship & Service Hymnal
Jesus Shall Reign	Watts/Hatton	CON	s	The Lutheran Hymnal
Jesus Shall Reign	Watts/Hatton	AUG	s	Lutheran Book Of Worship
Justice Shall Flourish	Everett Frese	NPM	s	Advent Psalms
Justice Shall Flourish	Angelo Della Picca	WLP	s	Cantor Book
Justice Shall Flourish	P. Cunningham	GRA	ht	
Justice Shall Flourish	Schiavone/Gelineau	GIA	st	Gelineau Gradual
Lord, Every Nation	W. A. Jurgens	OSB	s	Book Of Sacred Song
Lord, Every Nation	C. A. Peloquin	GIA	ao	Songs Of Israel
Lord, Every Nation	David C. Isele	GIA	as	Songs Of David
Lord, Every Nation	Proulx/Gelineau	GIA	st	Gelineau Gradual
Lord, Every Nation	Ron Ellis	RAV		
O God Bestow Your Judgment	S. Somerville	WLP	s	Psalms For Singing,Bk.2
O God By Your Judgment	William Callahan	ACP	s	Song Leader's Handbook

O God Give Your Judgment	Joseph Gelineau	GIA	s	30 Psalms & 2 Canticles
Proclaim To The World		ACP	s	The Johannine Hymnal
Sheaves Of Peace	F. Hillebrand	AHC	ast	Long Way Home
Shine, Arise In Your Splendor	Lucien Deiss	WLP	as	Alleluia, Sing W. New Songs
Today We Have Seen Your Glory	Douglas Mews	GIA	s	ICEL Lectionary Music
Wake, Awake	F. Mendelssohn	ACP	s	The Johannine Hymnal

73 ─────────────

From God Can Nothing Move	L. Helmbold	AUG	s	Lutheran Book Of Worship
How Good God Is	Joseph Gelineau	GIA	s	Grail-Gelineau Psalter
Jesus Thou Art Mine	Matthias Loy	CON	s	The Lutheran Hymnal
Surely God Loves Upright Men	Baughen/Seaman	GIA	s	Psalm Praise
Who Trusts In God	Magdeburg	CON	s	The Lutheran Hymnal
Who Trusts In God	Magdeburg/de Sermisy	AUG	s	Lutheran Book Of Worship
Why Should Cross And Trial	Gerhardt/Ebeling	CON	s	The Lutheran Hymnal

74 ─────────────

Go In Peace	Helmut Koenig	MPH	s	Suppl. To Book Of Hymns
Why O God Have You Cast Us Off	Joseph Gelineau	GIA	s	Grail-Gelineau Psalter

75 _____

Lord Every Nation	Christopher Willcock	PAA	ot	Psalms For Feasts & Seasons
We Give Thanks To You O God	Joseph Gelineau	GIA	s	Grail-Gelineau Psalter

76 _____

God Is Made Known	Joseph Gelineau	GIA	s	Grail-Gelineau Psalter
Grant Us Peace	Michael Gilligan	ACP	s	The Johannine Hymnal
Now Sing With Joy Jerusalem	H. T. Burleigh	ACP	s	The Johannine Hymnal
Shout Aloud To Heaven	Michael Gilligan	ACP	s	The Johannine Hymnal

77 _____

I Cry Aloud To God	Joseph Gelineau	GIA	s	Grail-Gelineau Psalter

78

Alleluia Christ Has Risen	John B. Dykes	ACP	s	The Johannine Hymnal
Do Not Forget	Batastini/Gelineau	GIA	st	Gelineau Gradual
Give Heed, My People	Joseph Gelineau	GIA	s	Grail-Gelineau Psalter
How Blessed Are They	J. H. Arnold	ACP	s	The Johannine Hymnal
How Blessed Are They	J. N. Brun	ACP	s	The Johannine Hymnal
In Ages Now Long Past	C. H. Graun	ACP	s	The Johannine Hymnal
In Ages Now Long Past	Michael Praetorius	ACP	s	The Johannine Hymnal
Let Children Hear	Watts/Cruger	CON	s	The Lutheran Hymnal
Praise The Lord	R. H. Pritchard	ACP	s	The Johannine Hymnal
The Glorious Deeds Of The Lord	P. Cunningham	GRA	ht	
The Lord Gave Them Bread	E. Diemente	WLP	s	Cantor Book
The Lord Gave Them Bread	Schiavone/Gelineau	GIA	st	Gelineau Gradual
What We Have Heard	William Callahan	ACP	s	Song Leader's Handbook

79

Lord Of Our Life	Lowenstern/Cruger	CON	s	The Lutheran Hymnal
Lord Of Our Life	von Lowenstern	AUG	s	Lutheran Book Of Worship
O God, The Nations	Joseph Gelineau	GIA	s	Grail-Gelineau Psalter
O Lord Be Not Mindful	Lucien Deiss	WLP		
O Mortal Man		ACP	s	The Johannine Hymnal

80

A Vine From Egypt	William Callahan	ACP	s	Song Leader's Handbook
Come, O Lord	Douglas Mews	GIA	s	ICEL Lectionary Music
Lord Make Us Turn To You	Robert Twynham	PAA	os	Psalms & Acclamations
Lord Make Us Turn To You	Joseph Gelineau	GIA	st	Gelineau Gradual
Lord Make Us Turn To You	R. S. Schaffer	WLP	s	Cantor Book
Lord, Make Us Turn To You	Everett Frese	NPM	s	Advent Psalms
Maranatha	Judy O'Sheil	FEL	s	Hymnal For Young Christians
O Shepherd Of Israel	Joseph Gelineau	GIA	s	30 Psalms & 2 Canticles
O Shepherd Of Israel	William Callahan	ACP		
Prayer...for Advent		ACP	s	The Johannine Hymnal
Save Us, O Lord	Tim Manion	NAL	ast	Lord Of Light
Savior, Like A Shepherd	Thrupp/Lindeman	AUG	s	Lutheran Book Of Worship
The Vineyard Of The Lord	Hughes/Gelineau	GIA	st	Gelineau Gradual
The Vineyard Of The Lord	Michael Lynch	RAV		
The Vineyard Of The Lord	P. Cunningham	GRA	ht	
The Vineyard Of The Lord	Robert Kreutz	WLP	s	Cantor Book

81

O Sing Joyfully	Adrian Batten	OXF	o	
Ring Out Your Joy To God	Joseph Gelineau	GIA	s	Worship II
Ring Out Your Joy To God	Joseph Gelineau	GIA	s	30 Psalms & 2 Canticles
Shout For Joy	Larry Florian	PAA	as	More Than The Sands
Sing Aloud Unto God	Robin Orr	OXF	o	
Sing We Merrily	Adrian Carpenter	OXF	o	
Sing We Merrily	Christopher Symons	OXF	o	
Sing With Joy To God	J. M. Burns	WLP	s	Cantor Book
Sing With Joy To God	P. Cunningham	GRA	ht	
Sing With Joy To God	Hughes/Gelineau	GIA	st	Gelineau Gradual
Take Up A Melody	William Callahan	ACP	s	Song Leader's Handbook

82

God Stands In The Divine Assembly	Joseph Gelineau	GIA	s	Grail-Gelineau Psalter
The Lord Will Come	John Milton	PIL	s	Pilgrim Hymnal
The Lord Will Come	John Milton	AUG	s	Lutheran Book Of Worship
The Lord Will Come	John Milton	CPF	s	The Hymnal 1940

83

| Psalm 83 | Juliana Garza | NAL | as | Communion Muse |
| O God, Do Not Keep Silent | Joseph Gelineau | GIA | s | Grail-Gelineau Psalter |

84

Blessed Are They	Noel Goemanne	GIA	s	ICEL Lectionary Music
Blessed Are They	Noel Goemanne	ICE	s	Music For The Rites
For Many Years	Czamanske/Nicolai	CON	s	The Lutheran Hymnal
Great God Attend	Watts/Venua	MPH	s	The Book Of Hymns
How Blessed Are They	J. H. Arnold	ACP	s	The Johannine Hymnal
How Blessed Are They	Martin Luther	ACP	s	The Johannine Hymnal
How Lovely	Richard Proulx	GIA	o	
How Lovely	Suzanne Toolan	GIA	ao	Living Spirit
How Lovely Are Thy Dwellings	J. Milton/J. Clark	PIL	s	Pilgrim Hymnal
How Lovely, How Lovely	Barnes/Wilson	GIA	s	Psalm Praise
How Lovely Is Thy Dwelling		MPH	s	The Book Of Hymns
How Lovely Is Your Dwelling	Owen Alstott	OCP	s	Choral Praise — 1985
How Lovely Is Your Dwelling	Randall DeBrun	OCP	s	Choral Praise — 1985
How Lovely Is Your Dwelling Place	Joseph Gelineau	GIA	s	Worship II
How Lovely Is Your Dwelling	C. A. Peloquin	GIA	o	
How Lovely Is Your Dwelling	H. B. Hays	OSB	s	Benedictine Book Of Song
How Lovely Is Your Dwelling	Joseph Gelineau	GIA	s	30 Psalms & 2 Canticles
How Lovely Is Your Dwelling	Michael Joncas	NAL	ast	On Eagle's Wings
How Lovely Is Your Dwelling	P. Cunningham	GRA	ht	
How Lovely Is Your Dwelling	Paul Lisicky	RPB	mt	Modern Liturgy,7.4
How Lovely Is Your Dwelling	S. Somerville	WLP	s	Psalms For Singing,Bk.1
How Lovely Is Your Dwelling	Westendorf/Vermulst	WLP	s	People's Mass Book
How Lovely Is Your Dwelling	Westendorf/Vermulst	WLP	s	People's Mass Book,1984

Lord Of The Worlds Above	Watts/Darwall	CON	s	The Lutheran Hymnal
Lovely Is Your Dwelling Place	James Marchionda	WLP	ast	Covenant
Morning Air Psalm	M. Williamson	BOH		
O Lord Of Hosts	Paul Quinlan	FEL	s	Hymnal For Young Christians
O How Amiable	Thomas Tompkins	OXF	o	
Pilgrimage Song	Helen Marie Gilsdorf	RPB	at	In The Breaking Of Bread
Pilgrimage Song	Helen Marie Gilsdorf	RPB	m	Modern Liturgy,8.5
Pleasant Are Thy Courts	Lyte/Gilbert	CPF	s	The Hymnal 1940
Shout Joyfully To God	Dave Brubeck	SFM	o	Mass - To Hope
The Sparrow Finds A Home	John Foley	NAL	as	Neither Silver Nor Gold
Your Dwelling Place	Steven Farney	RPB	amt	Modern Liturgy,12.7

85

Psalm 85	William Smith	OXF	o	
Come, O Lord	John Lee	OSB	s	Book Of Sacred Song
Come, O Lord	Christopher Willcock	GIA	s	ICEL Lectionary Music
Dona Nobis Pacem	Jacques Berthier	GIA	as	Music From Taize,2
I Will Hear	William Callahan	ACP	s	Song Leader's Handbook
Let Us See Your Kindness	Paul Lisicky	RPB	mt	Modern Liturgy,7.3
Lord Let Us See Your Kindness	Christopher Willcock	PAA	ot	Psalms For Feasts & Seasons
Lord Let Us See Your Kindness	Carroll/Gelineau	GIA	st	Gelineau Gradual
Lord Let Us See Your Kindness	Gerhard Track	OSB	s	Book Of Sacred Song
Lord Let Us See Your Kindness	Neil Blunt	WLP	s	Hundredfold
Lord, Let Us See Your Kindness	Joseph Roff	WLP	s	Psalms for the Cantor,1
Lord, Let Us See Your Kindness	Everett Frese	NPM	s	Advent Psalms
O Christe Domine Jesu	Jacques Berthier	GIA	as	Music From Taize,2
O Lord You Once Favored	Joseph Gelineau	GIA	s	30 Psalms & 2 Canticles
Peace To His People	P. Cunningham	GRA	ht	
Prayer For Peace	Joe Dailey	AHC	ast	Happy The Children
Seek First His Kingship	Denis Mullins	RPB	m	Modern Liturgy,10.8
The Lord Will Come	John Milton	CPF	s	The Hymnal 1940
The Lord Will Come	John Milton	PIL	s	Pilgrim Hymnal
The Voice Of God Speaks	Henry B. Hays	OSB	s	Benedictine Book Of Song
We Carry In Our Body	Tobias Colgan	ABB	ast	Songs Like Incense
When This Land Knew	Idle/Baughen	GIA	s	Psalm Praise
You Have Been Kind	S. Somerville	WLP	s	Psalms For Singing, Bk.2

86

Psalm 86	Jean Berger	FLA	o	
Psalm 86	John M. Talbot	CLM	ast	Come To The Quiet
Bow Down Thine Ear O Lord	William Hayes	OXF	o	
Lord You Are Good	Hughes/Gelineau	GIA	st	Gelineau Gradual
Lord You Are Good	R. J. Schaffer	WLP	s	Cantor Book
Mighty Lord	John Foley	NAL	as	Wood Hath Hope
Mighty Lord	John Foley	NAL	s	Glory And Praise,2
There's A Wideness	F. W. Faber	AUG	s	Lutheran Book Of Worship
Turn Your Ear, O Lord	Joseph Gelineau	GIA	s	Grail-Gelineau Psalter
Yahweh Is A Saving Lord	Roger Smith	NAL		A Song In My Heart
You O Lord	William Callahan	ACP	s	Song Leader's Handbook

87

Come Rich And Poor	Abbe Duguet	ACP	s	The Johannine Hymnal
Glories Of Your Name	Newton/F. J. Haydn	AUG	s	Lutheran Book Of Worship
O Sion, O My Mother	Lucien Deiss	WLP	at	Let The Earth Shout
O Sion, O My Mother	Lucien Deiss	WLP	s	Sing For The Lord
On The Holy Mountain	Joseph Gelineau	GIA	s	Grail-Gelineau Psalter
Psalm Of The City Of God	M. Williamson	BOH		

88

Come Thou Bright And Morning	Rosenroth	CON	s	The Lutheran Hymnal
Lord My God I Call For Help	Joseph Gelineau	GIA	s	Grail-Gelineau Psalter

89

Psalm 89	Joseph Gelineau	GIA	s	20 Psalms & 3 Canticles
Psalm 89	Karen Barrie Chapman	WLP	s	People's Mass Book,1984
Blessed Be The Lord Forever	Kent A. Newbury	WLP	o	
Eternal Father	John B. Dykes	ACP	s	The Johannine Hymnal
Forever I Will Sing	Everett Frese	NPM	s	Advent Psalms
Forever I Will Sing	Angelo Della Picca	WLP	s	Cantor Book
Forever I Will Sing	Carroll/Gelineau	GIA	st	Gelineau Gradual
Forever I Will Sing	Ellis & Lynch	RAV		
Forever I Will Sing	Howard Hughes	GIA	o	
Forever I Will Sing	Joe Zsigray	NAL	as	O Bless The Lord My Soul
Forever I Will Sing	P. Cunningham	GRA	ht	
Forever I Will Sing	Robert Twynham	GIA	o	
Happy Is The Man	Dan Schutte	NAL	as	Neither Silver Nor Gold
How Great And Good He Is	J. S. Bach	ACP	s	The Johannine Hymnal
I Have Made A Covenant	Karen Barrie	WGM	as	Songs Of Praise,1
I Have Made A Covenant	William Callahan	ACP	s	Song Leader's Handbook
I Will Sing Forever More	R. Knackal	OSB	s	Benedictine Book Of Song
Misericordias Domini	Jacques Berthier	GIA	as	Music From Taize,1
My Peace	Christopher Willcock	PAA	st	Let All The Peoples
Proclaim To The World		ACP	s	The Johannine Hymnal
The Favors Of The Lord	William Callahan	ACP	s	Song Leader's Handbook
The Son Of David	Hughes/Gelineau	GIA	st	Gelineau Gradual
The Son Of David	Robert Kreutz	WLP	s	Cantor Book
Timeless Love	Dudley-Smith/Warren	GIA	s	Psalm Praise
Yahweh The Holy One	Helen Marie Gilsdorf	RPB	mt	Modern Liturgy,6.2
Your Love O Lord	Peter Hallock	GIA	o	

90

Eternal Father, God Of Grace	Idle/Seaman	GIA	s	Psalm Praise
Fill Us With Your Love	Batastini/Gelineau	GIA	st	Gelineau Gradual
Fill Us With Your Love	Carolyn Cunningham	GRA	ht	
Fill Us With Your Love	P. Cunningham	GRA	ht	
Fill Us With Your Love	Angelo Della Picca	WLP	s	Cantor Book
Hear Us, Lord	Christopher Willcock	GIA	s	ICEL Lectionary Music
I Shall Sing Your Praises	Shawn Tracy	PAA	a	He Shall Be Peace
In Every Age, O Lord	Robert Kreutz	WLP	s	Cantor Book
In Every Age, O Lord	Peloquin/Gelineau	GIA	st	Gelineau Gradual
Lord, Give Success	J. M. Burns	WLP	s	Cantor Book
Lord, Thou Has Been Our Dwelling	Thomas Tallis	AUG	s	Psalms For The Church Year
O God Our Help In Ages Past	Watts/Croft	CON	s	The Lutheran Hymnal
O God Our Help In Ages Past	Watts/Croft	PIL	s	Pilgrim Hymnal
O God Our Help In Ages Past	Watts/Croft	CPF	s	The Hymnal 1940
O God Our Help In Ages Past	Watts/Croft	AUG	s	Lutheran Book Of Worship
O God, Our Help In Ages Past	Watts/Croft	HEL	s	The Catholic Liturgy Book
Remember Your Love	Balhoff/Ducote Et Al.	NAL	as	Remember Your Love
Remember Your Love	Balhoff/Ducote Et Al.	NAL	s	Glory And Praise,2
Teach Us	Steven Farney		mt	Modern Liturgy,12.6
Teach Us	William Callahan	ACP	s	Song Leader's Handbook
Thou Who Roll'st The Year	Ray Palmer	CON	s	The Lutheran Hymnal
We Come Unto Our Father's God	Thomas Gill	MPH	s	The Book Of Hymns
While With Ceaseless Course	John Newton	CON	s	The Lutheran Hymnal
Who Knows When Death	Juliane/Mock	CON	s	The Lutheran Hymnal
You Turn Man Back	William Callahan	ACP	s	Song Leader's Handbook

91

Psalm 91	Carol Dick	PAA	aos	In The Land Of The Living
Psalm 91	John M. Talbot	CLM	ast	Come To The Quiet
All Praise To Thee	Ken/Tallis	CON	s	The Lutheran Hymnal
Be With Me	Marty Haugen	GIA	s	Psalms For The Church Year
Be With Me	James J. Chepponis	WLP	s	Psalms For The Cantor,1
Be With Me	Michael Joncas	COO	ast	Every Stone Shall Cry
Be With Me Lord	Christopher Willcock	PAA	ot	Psalms For Feasts & Seasons
Be With Me Lord	Gerhard Track	OSB	s	Book Of Sacred Song
Be With Me Lord	Michael Joncas	WLP	s	People's Mass Book,1984
Be With Me Lord	Peloquin/Gelineau	GIA	st	Gelineau Gradual
Be With Me, Lord	M. Haugen	GIA	as	Gather To Remember
Be With Us	Marty Haugen	PAA	ast	With Open Hands
Blest Be The Lord	Dan Schutte	NAL	st	Glory And Praise,1
Blest Be The Lord	Dan Schutte	NAL	as	A Dwelling Place
He Who Dwells In The Shelter	Joseph Gelineau	GIA	s	Worship II
He Who Dwells In The Shelter	Joseph Gelineau	GIA	s	24 Psalms & A Canticle
He Will Keep You Safe	James Marchionda	WLP		
Now Let Us Come Before Him	Gerhardt, Kelly	CON	s	The Lutheran Hymnal
O You That Live	S. Somerville	WLP	s	Psalms For Singing,Bk. 1
On Eagle's Wings	Michael Joncas	NAL	s	Glory And Praise,2
On Eagle's Wings	Michael Joncas	NAL	ast	On Eagle's Wings
Praise To The Lord The Almighty	J. Neander	AUG	s	Lutheran Book Of Worship
Psalm Of God The Protector	M. Williamson	BOH		
Remember, O Lord	Douglas Mews	GIA	s	ICEL Lectionary Music
Safe In The Shadow	Dudley-Smith/Seaman	GIA	s	Psalm Praise
Savior Breathe An Eve. Blessing	Edmeston	CON	s	The Lutheran Hymnal
The Lord Is Near	W. A. Jurgens	OSB	s	Book Of Sacred Song
The Man Who Once	T. Tallis	PIL	s	Pilgrim Hymnal
The Man Who Once	T. Tallis	MPH	s	The Book Of Hymns
The Radiant Sun	Herman/Vulpius	CON	s	The Lutheran Hymnal
The Sun's Last Beam	N. Herman	CON	s	The Lutheran Hymnal
To His Angels	John Foley	NAL	as	Neither Silver Nor Gold
You Who Dwell	William Callahan	ACP	s	Song Leader's Handbook

92 ───────────────────────────────

Psalm 92	Edwin Fissinger	WLP	s	Three Sacred Anthems
Bonum Est Confidere	Jacques Berthier	GIA	as	Music From Taize,2
For You Make Me Glad	Dan Feiten	EKK	ast	For You Make Me Glad
Glory To The Father	Paul Quinlan	FEL	s	Hymnal For Young Christians
Great God We Sing	P. Doddridge	CON	s	The Lutheran Hymnal
How Good It Is	John Foley	NAL	as	Neither Silver Nor Gold
How Good To Offer Thanks	Chisholm/Schweizer	MPH	s	Suppl. To Book Of Hymns
How Great Thou Art	Carl Boberg	AUG	s	Lutheran Book Of Worship
It Is A Good Thing	David Hurd	GIA	o	Choral Series,1985
It Is Good	William Callahan	ACP	s	Song Leader's Handbook
It Is Good To Give Thanks	Robert Twynham	WGM	as	Songs Of Praise,1
Like Cedars They Shall Stand	Dan Schutte	NAL	s	Glory And Praise,2
Like Cedars They Shall Stand	Dan Schutte	NAL	as	Neither Silver Nor Gold
Lord It Is Good	Proulx/Gelineau	GIA	st	Gelineau Gradual
Lord It Is Good	Angelo Della Picca	WLP	s	Cantor Book
O Lord I Sing	Gerhardt, Kelly	CON	s	The Lutheran Hymnal
Sing Hosanna, Sing	Paul Quinlan	NAL		
Sweet Is The Work	Watts/Pleyel	HOP	s	The Service Hymnal
Worship And Praise	Jeffrey Keyes	RPB	mt	Modern Liturgy,5.5

93 ───────────────────────────────

Clothed In Kingly Majesty	Saward/Warren	GIA	s	Psalm Praise
Glorious Is The Lord On High	Howard Hughes	GIA	s	Praise God In Song
Sing We Praise	Perry /Warren	GIA	s	Psalm Praise
The Lord Is King	Carl Schalk	AUG	s	Psalms For The Church Year
The Lord Is King	Joseph Gelineau	GIA	s	24 Psalms & A Canticle
The Lord Is King	P. Cunningham	GRA	ht	
The Lord Is King	S. Somerville	WLP	s	Psalms For Singing,Bk.2
The Lord Is King	Batastini/Gelineau	GIA	st	Gelineau Gradual
The Lord Is King	J. G. Phillips	WLP	s	Cantor Book
The Lord Is King	Joseph Gelineau	GIA	s	Worship II
The Lord Reigns	Carl Schalk	AUG	s	Psalms For The Church Year
The Lord Shall Reign	David Hurd	GIA	o	Choral Series,1985
This Is My Father's World	Babcock/Sheppard	AUG	s	Lutheran Book Of Worship
You Servants Of God	Wesley/J. M. Haydn	AUG	s	Lutheran Book Of Worship

94

O Lord, Avenging God	Joseph Gelineau	GIA	s	Grail-Gelineau Psalter

95

Psalm 95	Allen Pote	CHO	o	
Psalm 95	Schutz/Reuning	GIA	s	Becker Psalter
Christ Is Born To Us	John Lee	OSB		
Come Let Us Sing	Paul Quinlan	FEL	s	Hymnal For Young Christians
Come Let Us Sing	William Callahan	ACP	s	Song Leader's Handbook
Come Let Us Worship	Eugene Englert	AUG	o	
Come Ring Out Your Joy	Joseph Gelineau	GIA	s	24 Psalms & A Canticle
Come Ring Out Your Joy	J. Coller	OSB	s	Benedictine Book Of Song
Come Sing Praises	Michael Perry	GIA	s	Psalm Praise
Come Sound His Praises	Watts/Wesley	MPH	s	The Book Of Hymns
Come Worship The Lord	John M. Talbot	CLM	ast	Come To The Quiet
Come, Lord Jesus	Everett Frese	NPM	s	Advent Psalms
Come, Let Us Sing	James Marchionda	WLP	ast	Covenant
Come, Let Us Worship	Shepherd/Englert	AUG	s	Seasonal Psalms
Festive Hymn Of Praise	Randall DeBruyn	OCP	s	Choral Praise — 1985
Follow The Saving Voice	Jack Miffleton	WLP	ast	Drylands
God Calling Yet!	Borthwick/Oliver	MPH	s	The Book Of Hymns
God Of Our Fathers	Faith Nardella	ACP	s	The Johannine Hymnal
Harden Not Your Hearts	Ron Ellis	RAV	as	Gentle Rains
If Today You Hear His Voice	David Haas	GIA	s	Psalms For The Church Year
If Today You Hear His Voice	David N. Johnson	WLP	s	Psalms For The Cantor,1
If Today You Hear His Voice	Robert E. Kreutz	OCP	o	
If Today You Hear His Voice	Owen Alstott	MLH	o	
If Today You Hear His Voice	Paul J. Prochaska	RPB	mt	Modern Liturgy,6.2
If Today You Hear His Voice	Tobias Colgan	ABB	ast	Songs Like Incense
If Today You Hear His Voice	Angelo Della Picca	WLP	o	
If Today You Hear His Voice	Carroll/Gelineau	GIA	st	Gelineau Gradual
If Today You Hear His Voice	Christopher Willcock	PAA	ot	Psalms For Feasts & Seasons
If Today You Hear His Voice	David C. Isele	GIA	as	Songs Of David
If Today You Hear His Voice	John Lee	OSB	s	Book Of Sacred Song
Let Us Open Our Lives	Marty Haugen	GIA	s	Gather Us In
Let Us Sing To The God	Bewes/Traditional	GIA	s	Psalm Praise
Lord Jesus Christ Be Present	Winkworth	CON	s	The Lutheran Hymnal
Lord Of My Life		CON	s	The Lutheran Hymnal
O Come And Sing To God	anon/Reinagle	HEL	s	The Catholic Liturgy Book
O Come Let Us Sing	Colin Mawby	GIA	s	Four Psalm Settings
O Come Let Us Sing	Thomas Tallis	AUG	s	Psalms For The Church Year
O Come Let Us Sing	Collins/Wilson	GIA	s	Psalm Praise
O Come Let Us Sing	David Harries	OXF	o	
O Come Let Us Sing	Gerhard Track	GIA	o	
O Come Let Us Sing	Seddon/Davies	GIA	s	Psalm Praise
Praise The Rock	Jan Vermulst	ACP	s	The Johannine Hymnal
Sanctus Dominus	Jacques Berthier	GIA	as	Music From Taize,2

Sing To The Lord A New Song	Douglas Mews	GIA	s	ICEL Lectionary Music
This Is The Day	Marty Haugen	PAA	ast	With Open Hands
To God With Gladness Sing	Quinn/Darwall	HEL	s	The Catholic Liturgy Book

96

A Song To The God We Love	Richard J. Meyette	RPB	mt	Modern Liturgy,11.5
Blessed Be The Lord	R. Vaughan Williams	ACP	s	The Johannine Hymnal
Christmas Midnight	Howard Hughes	GIA	o	
Earth And All Stars	Brokering/Johnson	AUG	s	Lutheran Book Of Worship
Give The Lord	C. Knoll/F.V.Strahan	HEL	s	The Catholic Liturgy Book
Give The Lord Glory	Michael Lynch	RAV		
Give The Lord Glory	Batastini/Gelineau	GIA	st	Gelineau Gradual
Give The Lord Glory	J. M. Burns	WLP	s	Cantor Book
Go And Teach All People	Robert Kreutz	ICE	s	Music For The Rites
Go Out To The World	Michael Joncas	NAL	ast	
Let All On Earth	Watts/Greiter	MPH	s	The Book Of Hymns
O Come All Ye Faithful	John F. Wade	ACP	s	The Johannine Hymnal
O Praise The Lord	Christopher Willcock	PAA	st	Let All The Peoples
O Sing A New Song	Joseph Gelineau	GIA	s	Worship II
O Sing A New Song	Joseph Gelineau	GIA	s	30 Psalms & 2 Canticles
O Sing Unto The Lord	William Mathias	OXF	o	
Proclaim His Marvelous Deeds	Joe Zsigray	NAL	as	Berakah
Proclaim His Marvelous Deeds	Joe Zsigray	NAL	s	Songs Of Praise & Reconcil.
Proclaim His Marvelous Deeds	Robert Twynham	GIA	o	
Proclaim His Marvelous Deeds	Batastini/Gelineau	GIA	st	Gelineau Gradual
Sanctus Dominus	Jacques Berthier	GIA	as	Music From Taize,2
Sing A New Song	James Blachura	RPB	st	Gather 'Round
Sing A New Song	J. Coller	OSB	s	Benedictine Book Of Song
Sing A New Song	C. Donahue	OSB	s	Benedictine Book Of Song
Sing To God A Joyous Song	Paul Quinlan	FEL	s	Hymnal For Young Christians
Sing To The Lord	William Callahan	ACP	s	Song Leader's Handbook
Sing To The Lord	S. Somerville	WLP	s	Psalms For Singing,Bk.2
Sing To The Lord	Saward/Wilson	GIA	s	Psalm Praise
Sing To The Lord	John Foley	NAL	as	Neither Silver Nor Gold
Sing To The Lord A New Song	Christopher Willcock	GIA	s	ICEL Lectionary Music
The Lord Is Come	Roger Petrich	CON	o	Choral Series 98-2596
The Lord Is Come	John Foley	NAL	as	Gentle Night
The Lord Will Come	John Milton	CPF	s	The Hymnal 1940
The Mountains Will Sing	J. M. Haydn	ACP	s	The Johannine Hymnal
The Royal Banners Forward Go	Fortunatus/Hampton	CON	s	The Lutheran Hymnal
The Royal Banners Forward Go	Fortunatus/Eccard	AUG	s	Lutheran Book Of Worship
This Is The Day	Robert Blue	FEL	s	Hymnal For Young Christians
Today Is Born	Angel Tucciarone	WLP	ast	Hundredfold

Today Is Born	Robert Twynham	PAA	o	Psalms & Acclamations
Today Is Born	Angelo Della Picca	WLP	s	Cantor Book
Today Is Born	C. A. Peloquin	GIA	o	
Today Is Born	Hughes/Gelineau	GIA	st	Gelineau Gradual
Worship And Praise	Jeffrey Keyes	RPB	mt	Modern Liturgy,5.5
Worship The Lord	Westendorf/Picca	WLP	s	People's Mass Book
Worship The Lord	M. H. Shepherd/W.Held	AUG	s	Seasonal Psalms
Worship The Lord	Wilbur Held	AUG	o	

97

Psalm 97	Tim Schoenbachler	NAL	a	Songs For The Masses
A Light Will Shine	Robert Kreutz	WLP	s	Cantor Book
A Light Will Shine	Carroll/Gelineau	GIA	st	Gelineau Gradual
Blessed Be The Lord	R. Vaughan Williams	ACP	s	The Johannine Hymnal
Come, Let Us Worship	Owen Alstott	OCP	s	Choral Praise — 1985
Praise The Lord	Mary S. A. Dougherty	RPB	st	Gather 'Round, Too
Rejoice, The Lord Is King	Tim Schoenbachler	NAL	a	O Jerusalem
Sing To The Lord	Owen Alstott	OCP	s	Choral Praise — 1985
Sing To The Lord	Owen Alstott	TMI	o	TM Choral Series
Sing To The Lord	Han Van Koert	ACP	s	The Johannine Hymnal
The Lord Is King	Idle/Warren	GIA	s	Psalm Praise
The Lord Is King	Joseph Gelineau	GIA		
The Lord Is King	Jeffrey Keyes	RPB	mt	Modern Liturgy,7.1
The Lord Is King	Proulx/Gelineau	GIA	st	Gelineau Gradual
The Lord Is King	William Callahan	ACP	s	Song Leader's Handbook
The Lord Is King	H. H. Smith	WLP	s	Cantor Book
The Lord Is King	Idle/Keys	GIA	s	Psalm Praise

Adaptation of Psalm 96

Sing a new song to the Lord!
His power, that moves all things
since the beginning,
has been manifested,
revealed to all eyes
and to the depths of our hearts.
Faithful to his ancient promises,
he defeated the enemies of our life.

Burst into music, O silent world,
let joy break through
and shake the earth with songs!
For the Lord of glory must be praised
throughout all distances of sky and land.
With the sound of trumpets and horns
celebrate the Lord!

Let the sea shout, let all waterways
be heard and let the hills
shout to each other in wind-songs!
For he comes to rule and to judge
with a measure beyond our understanding,
with the measure of his love!

Catherine de Vinck
©1975 Catherine de Vinck

98

Psalm 98	John Crawford	OXF	o	
Psalm 98	Schutz/Reuning	GIA	s	Becker Psalter
All Creatures Of Our God	Francis Of Assisi	AUG	s	Lutheran Book Of Worship
All The Ends	A. Gregory Murray	WLP	s	People's Mass Book,1984
All The Ends Of Earth	James V. Marchionda	WLP	s	Psalms For The Cantor,1
All The Ends Of The Earth	D. Haas & M. Haugen	GIA	s	Psalms For The Church Year
All The Ends Of The Earth	C. A. Peloquin	GIA	ao	Songs Of Israel
All The Ends Of The Earth	Christopher Willcock	PAA	ot	Psalms For Feasts & Seasons
All The Ends Of The Earth	David C. Isele	GIA	as	Songs Of David
All The Ends Of The Earth	Doug Hughes	RPB	mt	Modern Liturgy,5.7
All The Ends Of The Earth	J. Coller	OSB	s	Book Of Sacred Song
All The Ends Of The Earth	M. Zielenski	GIA	o	
All The Ends Of The Earth	Proulx/Gelineau	GIA	st	Gelineau Gradual
All The Ends Of The Earth	Bob Dufford	NAL	ast	Lord Of Light
All The Ends Of The Earth	D. Haas & M. Haugen	GIA	as	Psalms For The Church Year
Canta Aleluya	Jack Miffleton	WLP	ast	Drylands
His Saving Power Revealed	P. Cunningham	GRA	ht	
I Will Sing	Jeffrey Keyes	RPB	mt	Modern Liturgy,5.4
Joy To The World	Nelson	AUG	o	
Joy To The World	Watts/Handel	AUG	s	Lutheran Book Of Worship
Joy To The World	Watts/Handel	CON	s	The Lutheran Hymnal
Joy To The World	Watts/Handel	HOP	s	Worship & Service Hymnal
Joy To The World	Watts/Haweis	CPF	s	The Hymnal 1940
Joy To The World	Watts/Handel	HEL	s	The Catholic Liturgy Book
Joy To The World	Lowell Mason	ACP	s	The Johannine Hymnal
Let All The Earth	Rick Bennett	RPB	mt	Modern Liturgy,5.1
Lord, Today We Have Seen	W. A. Jurgens	OSB	s	Book Of Sacred Song
Make A Joyful Noise	M. Sindlinger	CHO	o	
Mountains And Hills	Dan Schutte	NAL	as	Neither Silver Nor Gold
New Songs Of Celebration	E.Routley/C.Young	AGA	oz	
O Sing Unto The Lord	William Mathias	OXF	o	
Shout Aloud To Heaven	Michael Gilligan	ACP	s	
Shout Out For Joy	C. A. Peloquin	GIA	ao	Missa A La Samba
Sing A New Song	Dudley-Smith/Davies	GIA	s	Psalm Praise
Sing A New Song	Dudley-Smith/Wilson	ERD	s	Sound Of Living Waters
Sing A New Song	Dudley-Smith/Wilson	GIA	s	Psalm Praise
Sing A New Song	Dudley-Smith/Wilson	GIA	s	Worship II
Sing A New Song	Joseph Gelineau	GIA	s	20 Psalms & 3 Canticles
Sing A New Song	Dan Schutte	NAL	as	Neither Silver Nor Gold
Sing A New Song	Dan Schutte	NAL	st	Glory And Praise,1
Sing Aloud Unto God	Robin Orr	OXF	o	
Sing Praise	William Callahan	ACP	s	Song Leader's Handbook
Sing To God New Songs	Baughen/Beethoven	GIA	s	Psalm Praise
Sing To The Lord	William Callahan	ACP	s	Song Leader's Handbook
Sing To The Lord	Angelo Della Picca	WP	s	Cantor Book
Sing To The Lord	Howard Hughes	GIA	o	
Sound Loud The Trumpet	Michael Perry	GIA	s	Psalm Praise
The Lord Comes To Rule	Peloquin/Gelineau	GIA	st	Gelineau Gradual
The Lord Comes To Rule	Robert Kreutz	WLP	s	Cantor Book
The Lord Has Revealed	Angelo Della Picca	WLP	s	Cantor Book
The Lord Has Revealed	Proulx/Gelineau	GIA	st	Gelineau Gradual

The Strife Is O'er	Pott/Palestrina	CON	s	The Lutheran Hymnal
This Is My Father's World	Babcock/Sheppard	AUG	s	Lutheran Book Of Worship
This Is The Day/Psallite Deo	Jacques Berthier	GIA	a	Music From Taize,2
To God We Sing A New Song	Michael Gilligan	ACP	s	The Johannine Hymnal
To Yahweh Sing A New Song	Agnes Meysenberg	GIA	s	Worship II
Today We Have Seen Your Glory	Christopher Willcock	GIA	s	ICEL Lectionary Music

99 _____

Cry Out With Joy	Christopher Walker	OXF	o	
God Is King	Saward/Baughen	GIA	s	Psalm Praise
Holy, Holy Is The Lord	Paul Quinlan	FEL	s	Hymnal For Young Christians
The Lord Is King	Francis A. Wapen	GIA	o	
The Lord Is King	Joseph Gelineau	GIA	s	20 Psalms & 3 Canticles

100 _____

Psalm 100	C. A. Peloquin	GIA	ao	Songs Of Israel
Psalm 100	Schutz/Reuning	GIA	s	Becker Psalter
Psalm 100	Zimmermann	AUG	o	
All People That On Earth Do Dwell	Kethe/Bourgeois	AUG	s	Lutheran Book Of Worship
All People That On Earth Do Dwell	Kethe/Bourgeois	GIA	s	Worship II
All People That On Earth Do Dwell	Kethe/Bourgeois	PIL	s	Pilgrim Hymnal
All People That On Earth Do Dwell	Kethe/Bourgeois	WLP	s	People's Mass Book,1984
All People That On Earth Do Dwell	Kethe/Hampton	GIA	s	Worship II
All People That On Earth Do Dwell	William Kethe	CON	s	The Lutheran Hymnal
All People That On Earth Do Dwell	William Kethe	CPF	s	The Hymnal 1940
All The Earth	Lucien Deiss	WLP	a	With Joyful Lips
All The Earth	Lucien Deiss	WLP	s	Biblical Hymns & Psalms,1
All The Earth	Lucien Deiss	WLP	s	People's Mass Book
All The Earth	Lucien Deiss	WLP	s	People's Mass Book,1984
Be Joyful In The Lord	Beach/Friedell	PIL	s	Pilgrim Hymnal

Be Joyful In The Lord	Brian Longthorne	OXF	o	
Be Joyful In The Lord	Healy Willan	OXF	o	
Be Joyful In The Lord	John Nourse	OXF	o	
Before Jehovah's Awe-ful Throne	Isaac Watts	CON	s	The Lutheran Hymnal
Before Jehovah's Aweful Throne	Watts/Bourgeois	MPH	s	The Book Of Hymns
Before Jehovah's Aweful Throne	Watts/Venua	PIL	s	Pilgrim Hymnal
Before Jehovah's Awesome Throne	Watts/Bourgeois	AUG	s	Lutheran Book Of Worship
Come Rejoice	Baughen/Tredinnick	GIA	s	Psalm Praise
Come Rejoice	Baughen/Tredinnick	GIA	s	Worship II
Come Rejoice	Baughen/Wilson	GIA	s	Psalm Praise
Cry Out With Joy	Joseph Gelineau	GIA	s	24 Psalms & A Canticle
Cry Out With Joy	Joseph Gelineau	GIA	s	Worship II
Enter His Gates	Richard Hillert	AUG	o	
Enter His Gates	Shepherd/Hillert	AUG	s	Seasonal Psalms
How Great And Good He Is	J. S. Bach	ACP	s	The Johannine Hymnal
In Praise Of His Name	Roc O'Connor	NAL	as	A Dwelling Place
In Praise Of His Name	Roc O'Connor	NAL	st	Glory And Praise,2
Joy In The Lord	Jane Trigg	ERD	s	Sound Of Living Waters
Jubilate Everybody	Michael Perry	GIA	s	Psalm Praise
Lands Of The Earth	Collins/Warren	GIA	s	Psalm Praise
Let All The Earth Cry Out	S. Somerville	WLP	s	People's Mass Book
Lord Jesus, Come	C. A. Peloquin	GIA	ao	Lyric Liturgy
Make A Joyful Noise	Judy Hunnicutt	AUG	o	
Make A Joyful Noise	Eric Goosen	SOM	o	
Make A Joyful Noise	Johann Schein	AUG	s	Psalms For The Church Year
Mighty Lord	John Foley	NAL	as	Wood Hath Hope
O God Of Light	Taylor/Cabena	AUG	s	Lutheran Book Of Worship
O My Soul Bless God The Father		PIL	s	Pilgrim Hymnal
O Sing Jubilee	Koren/Hoff	AUG	s	Lutheran Book Of Worship
Open Now Thy Gates	Schmolk/Neander	AUG	s	Lutheran Book Of Worship
Open Thy Gates Of Beauty	Winkworth/Neander	CON	s	The Lutheran Hymnal
Praise The Lord	J. Coller	OSB	s	Book Of Sacred Song
Shout To The Lord	Jean Berger	CFP		
Sing All Creation	C. Donohue	OSB	s	Benedictine Book Of Song
Sing Joyfully	William Callahan	ACP	s	Song Leader's Handbook
Sing Joyfully To The Lord	Joseph Roff	GIA	o	
The Lord Be With You	Paul Quinlan	FEL	s	Hymnal For Young Christians
We Are His People	David Haas	GIA	s	Psalms For The Church Year
We Are His People	Suzanne Toolan	WLP	s	Psalms For The Cantor,1
We Are His People	C. P. Mudd	PAA	s	Daily Praise
We Are His People	Kremer/Gelineau	GIA	st	Gelineau Gradual
We Are His People	W. A. Jurgens	OSB	s	Book Of Sacred Song
We Are His People	P. Cunningham	GRA	ht	
We Are His People	R. C. Verdi	GIA	o	
We Are His People	R. LeBlanc	OSB	s	Benedictine Book Of Song
We Are His People	Christopher Willcock	PAA	ot	Psalms For Feasts & Seasons
We Are The People	Jack Miffleton	WLP	ast	Drylands
Ye Lands To The Lord	Koren/Hoff	CON	s	The Lutheran Hymnal
You Are My Friends	Donald J. Reagan	NAL	s	Glory And Praise,2
You Are My Friends	Theophane Hytrek	GIA	s	ICEL Lectionary Music
You Are My Friends	Theophane Hytrek	ICE	s	Music For The Rites

101_____

Mighty Lord	John Foley	NAL	s	Glory And Praise,2
My Song Is Of Mercy	Joseph Gelineau	GIA	s	Grail-Gelineau Psalter
My Song Shall Be Of Mercy	Colin Mawby	GIA	s	Four Psalm Settings

102_____

Psalm 102	Schutz/Reuning	GIA	s	The Becker Psalter
Answer When I Call	John Foley	NAL	ast	Lord Of Light
Come Let Us Return	Columba Kelly Et Al.	ABB	as	Remaining Faithful
Let All The Peoples	Christopher Willcock	PAA	st	Let All The Peoples
My Days Are Gone	John Blow	OXF	o	
O Lord, Hear My Prayer	Jacques Berthier	GIA	as	Music From Taize,2
O Lord, Listen To My Prayer	Joseph Gelineau	GIA	s	Grail-Gelineau Psalter
The Love Of The Lord	Columba Kelly Et Al.	ABB	ast	Songs Like Incense

103_____

Psalm 103	Cain	FLA	o	
Psalm 103	J. Hamm, D. Mansheim	PAA	ast	The Works Of God
Psalm 103	Michael Lynch	RAV	as	Gentle Rains
Abba, Father	Ellen Marie Keating	WLP	s	People's Mass Book,1984
All Of My Life	Mary Grace Zunic	FEL	s	Hymnal For Young Christians
Bless The Lord	Edward Walker	WRD		
Bless The Lord	Jacques Berthier	GIA	as	Music From Taize,2
Bless The Lord		ACP	s	The Johannine Hymnal
Bless The Lord	Dan Feiten	EKK	ast	For You Make Me Glad
Bless The Lord	William Callahan	ACP	s	Song Leader's Handbook
Bless The Lord, My Soul	J. S. Bach	FLA	o	
Bless The Lord, My Soul	Randall DeBruyn	WLP	s	Psalms For The Cantor,1
Bless The Lord O My Soul	Ippolitov-Ivanov	GIA	o	
Bless The Lord O My Soul	J. Poliander	AUG	s	Psalms For The Church Year
Bless The Lord O My Soul	Michael Baughen	GIA	s	Psalm Praise

Bless Thou The Lord	B. Pulkingham	ERD	s	Sound Of Living Waters
How Good Is The Lord	Carey Landry	NAL	a	I Will Not Forget You
How Great And Good Is He	J. S. Bach	ACP	s	The Johannine Hymnal
Monsoon Rain	F. Hillebrand	AHC	ast	Long Way Home
My Soul Give Thanks	Joseph Gelineau	GIA	s	30 Psalms & 2 Canticles
My Soul Give Thanks	Joseph Gelineau	GIA	s	Worship II
My Soul Give Thanks	Proulx/Gelineau	GIA	o	
My Soul Now Bless Thy Maker	C. Winkworth	CON	s	The Lutheran Hymnal
My Soul Now Praise Your Maker	Gramann	AUG	s	Lutheran Book Of Worship
O Lord Be Not Mindful	Lucien Deiss	WLP		
O Bless The Lord	P. Cunningham	GRA	ht	
O Bless The Lord My Soul	S. Somerville	WLP	s	Psalms For Singing,Bk.2
O Bless The Lord My Soul	Montgomery, Wesley	CPF	s	The Hymnal 1940
O Bless The Lord, My Soul	Montgomery/Williams	HEL	s	The Catholic Liturgy Book
O My Soul Bless God	G. F. Handel	FLA	o	
O My Soul Bless God		MPH	s	The Book Of Hymns
Oh Bless The Lord My Soul	Watts/Williams	CON	s	The Lutheran Hymnal
Our Help	Oosterhuis/Huijbers	NAL	as	When From Our Exile
Praise My Soul The King Of Heave	Lyte/Goss	GPH	s	Hymns Of Glorious Praise
Praise My Soul The King Of Heave	Lyte/Goss	CPF	s	The Hymnal 1940
Praise My Soul The King Of Heave	Lyte/Goss	PIL	s	Pilgrim Hymnal
Praise My Soul The King Of Heave	Lyte/Goss	WLP	s	People's Mass Book
Praise My Soul The King Of Heave	Lyte/Smart	MPH	s	The Book Of Hymns
Praise My Soul The King Of Heave	Lyte/Goss	HEL	s	The Catholic Liturgy Book
Praise My Soul The King Of Heave	Lyte/Goss	AUG	s	Lutheran Book Of Worship
Praise The Lord	H. J. Gauntlett	ACP	s	The Johannine Hymnal
Praise The Lord	John Goss	ACP	s	The Johannine Hymnal
Praise The Lord O My Soul	Thomas Tompkins	OXF		
Praise The Lord My Soul	John Foley	NAL	as	Earthen Vessels
Praise The Lord My Soul	John Foley	NAL	st	Glory And Praise,1
Praise To The Lord	Joachim Neander	HEL	s	The Catholic Liturgy Book
Praise To The Lord The Almighty	J. Neander	CPF	s	The Hymnal 1940
Praise To The Lord The Almighty	J. Neander	AUG	s	Lutheran Book Of Worship
Sing To The Lord	Gerhard Track	OSB	s	Book Of Sacred Song
The Lord Has Set His Throne	Kreutz/Gelineau	GIA	st	Gelineau Gradual
The Lord Has Set His Throne	Angelo Della Picca	WLP	s	Cantor Book
The Lord Is Kind	Donald J. Reagan	WLP	s	Psalms For The Cantor,1
The Lord Is Kind	Iverson/Thiel	RPB	mt	Modern Liturgy,5.8
The Lord Is Kind	J. M. Burns	WLP	s	Cantor Book
The Lord Is Kind	Peloquin/Gelineau	GIA	st	Gelineau Gradual
The Lord Is Kind	Batastini/Gelineau	GIA	st	Gelineau Gradual
The Lord Is Kind	Christopher Willcock	PAA	ot	Psalms For Feasts & Seasons
The Lord Is Kind	H. H. Smith	WLP	s	Cantor Book
The Lord Is Kind and Merciful	Marty Haugen	GIA	s	Psalms For The Church Year
The Lord Is Kind And Merciful	Noel Goemanne	GIA	s	ICEL Lectionary Music
The Lord's Kindness	Robert Kreutz	WLP	s	Cantor Book
The Lord's Kindness	Batastini/Gelineau	GIA	st	Gelineau Gradual
The Spirit Of The Lord	Robert Twynham	PAA	o	Psalms & Acclamations
You Can Fly	Michael Lynch	NAL	ast	Starlight

104

Psalm 104		WLP		
Bless The Lord	Edward Walker	WRD	s	Pilgrim Praise
Bless The Lord	William Callahan	ACP	s	Song Leader's Handbook
Bless The Lord My Soul	Joseph Gelineau	GIA	s	20 Psalms & 3 Canticles
I Want To Call You	Oosterhuis/Huijbers	NAL	as	When From Our Exile
I Will Bless You	Howard Hughes	ICE	s	Consult, On A Liturgical Psalt
I Will Sing Unto The Lord	John Amner	OXF	o	
In Majesty And Splendour	Perry/Warren	GIA	s	Psalm Praise
Let All Creation	Haldan Tompkins	WLP	s	People's Mass Book
Let All Creation	Haldan Tompkins	WLP	s	People's Mass Book,1984
Lord, Send Out Your Spirit	Richard T. Proulx	WLP	s	Psalms For The Cantor,1
Lord, Send Out Your Spirit	David Haas	GIA	s	Psalms For The Church Year
Lord, Send Out Your Spirit	Dean Olawski	WRD		
Lord, Send Out Your Spirit	Angelo Della Picca	WLP	o	
Lord, Send Out Your Spirit	Balhoff/Daigle Et Al.	NAL	as	Path Of Life
Lord, Send Out Your Spirit	C. A. Peloquin	GIA	ao	Songs Of Israel
Lord, Send Out Your Spirit	Christopher Willcock	PAA	ot	Psalms For Feasts & Seasons
Lord, Send Out Your Spirit	Ellis & Lynch	RAV	as	With All My Heart
Lord, Send Out Your Spirit	G. Farrell	OSB	s	Book Of Sacred Song
Lord, Send Out Your Spirit	Neil Blunt	WLP	ast	Hundredfold
Lord, Send Out Your Spirit	Proulx/Gelineau	GIA	st	Gelineau Gradual
Lord, Send Out Your Spirit	Robert Smith	GIA	o	
Lord, Send Out Your Spirit	Ronald Arnatt	GIA	s	ICEL Lectionary Music
Lord, Send Out Your Spirit	J. Zsigray	NAL	ast	Father, We Sing Your Praises
Lord, Send Your Spirit	Robert Mondoy	RPB	st	Gather 'Round, Too
O Worship The King	Grant/J. M. Haydn	PIL	s	Pilgrim Hymnal
O Worship The King	Grant/Croft	HEL	s	The Catholic Liturgy Book
O Worship The King	Grant/Croft	CPF	s	The Hymnal 1940
Oh, Worship The King	Grant/Croft	AUG	s	Lutheran Book Of Worship
Oh, Worship The King	Robert Grant	CON	s	The Lutheran Hymnal
Psalm For Pentecost	Eileen Freeman	RPB	mt	Worship Times,1.2
Psalm Of Thanksgiving	Harold Darke	OXF	o	
Send Out Your Spirit	Tim Schoenbachler	PAA	ast	All Is Ready
Spirit Of Love	Jack Miffleton	WLP	ast	Drylands
Thank You, Lord, For Water	Wren/Routley	MPH	s	Suppl. To Book Of Hymns
The Earth Is Full	Roberta McGrath	RPB	st	Gather 'Round
The Earth Is Full	Angelo Della Picca	WLP	s	Cantor Book
We Praise You, O Lord	G. Farrell	OSB	s	Book Of Sacred Song

105

Give Thanks To The Lord	Joseph Gelineau	GIA	s	Grail-Gelineau Psalter
His Love Will Ever Be	Bob Fabing	NAL	ast	Song Of The Lamb
Lift Up Your Hearts	Seddon/Warren	GIA	s	Psalm Praise
O Give Thanks Unto The Lord	Thomas Tompkins	OXF	o	
O Give Thanks	Frederic Goossen	SOM	o	
O Heaven Hear Me	Henry Carey	ACP	s	The Johannine Hymnal
Praise The Lord Sing To Yahweh	P. Cunningham	PAS	st	Cast Into The Deep
Rejoice In The Lord	James V. Marchionda	WLP	s	People's Mass Book,1984
Thanks Be To Yahweh	Schutz/Reuning	GIA	s	Becker Psalter
Thanks Be To Yahweh	Schutz/Reuning	GIA	s	Worship II

106

Come You Faithful	Johann Roh	ACP	s	The Johannine Hymnal
For Unity	C. A. Peloquin	GIA	o	
Give Thanks	Paul Lisicky	RPB	mt	Modern Liturgy,6.4
Give Thanks To The Lord	Joseph Gelineau	GIA	s	Grail-Gelineau Psalter
Heed My Call For Help	John Foley	NAL	as	
Love Divine	Charles Wesley	CON	s	The Lutheran Hymnal
O Heaven Hear Me	Henry Carey	ACP	s	The Johannine Hymnal
Praise And Thanks	Thomas H. Kingo	AUG	s	Lutheran Book Of Worship
Praise To Thee	Thomas H. Kingo Et Al.	CON	s	The Lutheran Hymnal
See How The Lord Blesses	James J. Chepponis	GIA	o	
Send Forth Your Word	Robert Kreutz	GIA	o	

107

Title	Composer	Pub	Type	Source
Give Thanks To The Lord	Angelo Della Picca	WLP	s	Cantor Book
Give Thanks To The Lord	Carroll/Gelineau	GIA	st	Gelineau Gradual
Give Thanks To The Lord	P. Cunningham	GRA	ht	
Give Thanks To The Lord	Saward/Keys	GIA	s	Psalm Praise
How Brightly Shines	C. H. Graun	ACP	s	The Johannine Hymnal
O Give Thanks To The Lord	Joseph Gelineau	GIA	s	20 Psalms & 3 Canticles
O Lord Our Father Thanks	Schneegass, Crull	CON	s	The Lutheran Hymnal
Peace Is Flowing Like A River	Carey Landry	NAL	as	I Will Not Forget You
Proclaim To The World		ACP	s	The Johannine Hymnal
They Who Sailed	Joseph Gelineau	GIA	s	20 Psalms & 3 Canticles

108

Title	Composer	Pub	Type	Source
Awake, My Soul	Ken/Barthelemon	CON	s	The Lutheran Hymnal
Awake, My Soul	Ken/Barthelemon	AUG	s	Lutheran Book Of Worship
My Heart Is Ready	Joseph Gelineau	GIA	s	Grail-Gelineau Psalter
Oh Praise The Lord My Soul	Wright/Anders	AUG	s	Lutheran Book Of Worship
Wake Up, My Soul	Hal H. Hopson	CFS	o	

109

Title	Composer	Pub	Type	Source
O God Whom I Praise	Joseph Gelineau	GIA	s	Grail-Gelineau Psalter
O Lord God	Mary Grace Zunic	FEL	s	Hymnal For Young Christians
Yours Is Princely Power	Joe Wise	PAA	a	Hand In Hand

110

Battle Hymn Of The Republic	Julia Ward Howe	ACP	s	The Johannine Hymnal
Christ The Lord, A Priest	Theophane Hytrek	ICE	s	Music For The Rites
Savior Again To Thy Dear Name	Ellerton/Hopkins	CON	s	The Lutheran Hymnal
The Lord Said	William Callahan	ACP	s	Song Leader's Handbook
The Lord's Revelation	Joseph Gelineau	GIA	s	20 Psalms & 3 Canticles
Yahweh Said To My Lord	S. Somerville	WLP	s	Psalms For Singing,Bk.2
You Are A Priest	Batastini/Gelineau	GIA	st	Gelineau Gradual
You Are A Priest	J. G. Phillips	WLP	s	Cantor Book
You Are A Priest	P. Cunningham	GRA	ht	
You Are A Priest Forever	Theophane Hytrek	GIA	s	ICEL Lectionary Music

111

I Thank You Lord	Michael Saward	GIA	s	Psalm Praise
I Will Exalt The Lord	S. Somerville	WLP	s	Psalms For Singing,Bk.2
I Will Thank The Lord	Joseph Gelineau	GIA	s	20 Psalms & 3 Canticles
With All My Heart	Paul Lisicky	RPB	mt	Modern Liturgy,6.2

112

A Light In Darkness	P. Cunningham	GRA	ht	
He Shall Stand Fast	Suzanne Toolan	RPB	ast	Keeping Feastival
He Who Stands In Awe	Saward/Warren	GIA	s	Psalm Praise
How Happy Is The Man	S. Somerville	WLP	s	Psalms For Singing,Bk.2
Processional	Suzanne Toolan	RPB	mt	Modern Liturgy,4.8
The Just Man Is A Light	H. H. Smith	WLP	s	Cantor Book
The Just Man Is A Light	Proulx/Gelineau	GIA	st	Gelineau Gradual
The Lord Dawns	William Callahan	ACP	s	Song Leader's Handbook

113_____

Blessed Be The Name Of The Lord	H. H. Smith	WLP	s	Cantor Book
Blest Be The Name Of The Lord	Paul Quinlan	FEL	s	Hymnal For Young Christians
Give Praise To The Lord	Lucien Deiss	ACP	s	The Johannine Hymnal
Give Praise You Servants	S. Somerville	WLP	s	Psalms For Singing,Bk.2
O Trinity, O Blessed Light	St. Ambrose/Herman	AUG	s	Lutheran Book Of Worship
Praise God	Mischke/Lindusky	WLP	s	People's Mass Book,1984
Praise O Servants	Joseph Gelineau	GIA	s	30 Psalms & 2 Canticles
Praise His Name	Michael Joncas	NAL	ast	On Eagle's Wings
Praise The Lord	David C. Isele	GIA	s	Praise God In Song
Praise The Lord	John Blow	OXF	o	
Praise The Lord	M. Fautch	WLP	s	Cantor Book
Praise The Lord	Paul Quinlan	WLP	a	Glory Bound
Praise The Lord	Peloquin/Gelineau	GIA	st	Gelineau Gradual
Praise Ye The Lord	Christopher Tye	OXF	o	
Praise Ye The Lord	Gordon Young	OXF	o	
Praise You Servants	R. Hutmacher	GIA	o	
Praise You Servants	William Callahan	ACP	s	Song Leader's Handbook
The Day Thou Gavest	Ellerton/Bourgeois	MPH	s	The Book Of Hymns

114_____

Israel Has Gone Out Of Egypt	S. Somerville	WLP	s	Psalms For Singing,Bk.2
Israel Went Out From Egypt	Paul Quinlan	FEL	s	Hymnal For Young Christians
Tremble, Tremble Little Earth	Paul Quinlan	WLP		
When Israel Came Forth	Joseph Gelineau	GIA	s	20 Psalms & 3 Canticles
Yes, I Will Arise	Suzanne Toolan	RPB	st	Gather 'Round, Too

115

His Love Will Ever Be	Bob Fabing	NAL s	Glory And Praise,2
Israel Has Gone Out Of Egypt	S. Somerville	WLP s	Psalms For Singing,Bk.2
Not To Us	Oosterhuis/Huijbers	NAL as	When From Our Exile
Not To Us Be Glory Given	Dudley-Smith/Jones	GIA s	Psalm Praise
Not To Us, Lord	Joseph Gelineau	GIA s	Grail-Gelineau Psalter
Not To Us, O Lord	Paul Quinlan	FEL s	Hymnal For Young Christians

116

How Shall I Make	William Callahan	ACP s	Song Leader's Handbook
I Believed	William Callahan	ACP s	Song Leader's Handbook
I Love The Lord	Barnes Et Al./Wilson	GIA s	Psalm Praise
I Love The Lord	Joseph Gelineau	GIA s	24 Palms & A Canticle
I Love The Lord	Kuipers/Maitr.Pierre	HOP s	The Service Hymnal
I Love The Lord	William Callahan	ACP s	Song Leader's Handbook
I Trusted Even When I Said	Joseph Gelineau	GIA s	24 Psalms & A Canticle
I Will Take The Cup	Angelo Della Picca	WLP s	Cantor Book
I Will Take The Cup	Murray/Gelineau	GIA st	Gelineau Gradual
I Will Walk In The Presence	Donald Reagan	NAL ast	You Are My Friends
I Will Walk In The Presence	Howard Hughes	WLP s	Cantor Book
I Will Walk In The Presence	Proulx/Gelineau	GIA st	Gelineau Gradual
In The Presence	Ellis & Ellis	RAV h	
O Lord My God	Selnecker	CON s	The Lutheran Hymnal
Our Blessing Cup	Marty Haugen	GIA s	Psalms For The Church Year
Our Blessing Cup	Michael Joncas	NAL s	Glory And Praise,2
Our Blessing Cup	Michael Joncas	NAL ast	On Eagle's Wings
Our Blessing Cup	P. Cunningham	GRA ht	
Our Blessing Cup	Peloquin/Gelineau	GIA st	Gelineau Gradual
Our Blessing Cup	Angelo Della Picca	WLP s	Cantor Book
Song For Liz	Jeffrey Keyes	RPB mt	Modern Liturgy,7.1
The Cup Of Salvation	Phyllis Warner	AUG o	Choral Settings 11-4622
What Shall I Render?	Margaret Douroux	ABI s	Songs Of Zion
Yes, I Will Arise	Suzanne Toolan	RPB st	Gather 'Round, Too
You Will Show Me The Path	Joe Zsigray	NAL as	Berakah

117

Psalm 117	Harold Shapero	SOM	s	Two Psalms
Psalm 117	Marano	FLA	o	
Psalm 117	Roger Sherman	GIA	o	
All The Nations	S. Somerville	WLP	s	Psalms For Singing,Bk.2
From All That Dwell	Watts/Bourgeois	AUG	s	Lutheran Book Of Worship
From All That Dwell	Watts/Bourgeois	PIL	s	Pilgrim Hymnal
From All That Dwell	Watts/Bourgeois	CPF	s	The Hymnal 1940
From All That Dwell	Isaac Watts	CON	s	The Lutheran Hymnal
From All That Dwell	Watts/Hatton	MPH	s	The Book Of Hymns
From All That Dwell	Watts, Ken/Bourgeois	HEL	s	The Catholic Liturgy Book
Go Out And Tell The News	P. Cunningham	GRA	ht	
Go Out To All The World	H. H. Smith	WLP	s	Cantor Book
Go Out To All The World	Peloquin/Gelineau	GA	st	Gelineau Gradual
Holy Is God	David C. Isele	GIA	s	Praise God In Song
Holy Is God	Howard Hughes	GIA	s	Praise God In Song
Holy Is God	Michael Joncas	GIA	s	Praise God In Song
Laudate Dominum	Jacques Berthier	GIA	as	Music From Taize,1
Laudate Dominum		GIA	s	Worship II
O Praise The Lord	Joseph Gelineau	GIA	s	Worship II
O Praise The Lord	Joseph Gelineau	GIA	s	24 Psalms & A Canticle
O Praise The Lord	Joseph Gelineau	GIA	s	20 Psalms & 3 Canticles
O Praise The Lord	L. Mason	GIA	o	
Praise God with Sound	Heinrich Schutz	BBL		
Praise The Lord	Carl Schalk	AUG	s	Psalms For The Church Year
Praise The Lord	Caldara/Tortolano	GIA	o	
Praise The Lord	William Callahan	ACP	s	Song Leader's Handbook

118

All Glory, Laud And Honor	Theodulph Of Orleans	AUG	s	Lutheran Book Of Worship
Alleluia	Balhoff/Daigle Et Al.	NAL	as	Path Of Life
Behold The Sure Foundation	Watts/Croft	CON	s	The Lutheran Hymnal
Christus Resurrexit	Jacques Berthier	GIA	as	Music From Taize,2
Demos Gracias(We Give Thanks)	Trad. Hispanic,tr.E.Fra	MPH	s	Suppl. To Book Of Hymns
Give Thanks To The Lord	Robert Twynham	PAA	o	Psalms & Acclamations
Give Thanks To The Lord	William Callahan	ACP	s	Song Leader's Handbook
Give Thanks To The Lord		ACP	s	The Johannine Hymnal
Give Thanks To The Lord	Angelo Della Picca	WLP	s	Cantor Book
Give Thanks To The Lord	Carroll/Gelineau	GIA	st	Gelineau Gradual
Glory Hosanna		ACP	s	The Johannine Hymnal
Greet The Risen Lord	Jack Miffleton	ACP	s	The Johannine Hymnal

Let The House	William Callahan	ACP	s	Song Leader's Handbook
Let Us Rejoice	Marty Haugen	GIA	s	Psalms For The Church Year
My Inmost Heart	Nigidius	CON	s	The Lutheran Hymnal
O Lord we Praise Thee	Martin Luther	CON	s	The Lutheran Hymnal
O Day Of Rest And Gladness	C. Wordsworth	CON	s	The Lutheran Hymnal
Oh, Sing with Exultation	Arrebo, Doving	CON	s	The Lutheran Hymnal
Praise The Lord	Howard Hughes	GIA	s	Praise God In Song
Praise To The Lord	Idle/Warren	GIA	s	Psalm Praise
Rendez A Dieu	Claude Goudimel	GIA	o	Ars Antiqua Chorialis
Sing To The Mountains	Bob Dufford	NAL	st	Glory And Praise,1
Sing To The Mountains	Bob Dufford	NAL	as	Earthen Vessels
Surrexit Christus	Jacques Berthier	GIA	as	Music From Taize,2
The Day Of Resurrection	John Of Damascus	AUG	s	Lutheran Book Of Worship
The Day Of Resurrection	John Of Damascus	CON	s	The Lutheran Hymnal
The Hand Of The Lord	Gregory Norbet	WES	ast	Spirit Alive
The Right Hand Of The Lord	William Shafer	ACP	s	The Johannine Hymnal
The Stone Rejected	Angelo Della Picca	WLP	s	Cantor Book
The Stone Rejected	Carrol/Gelineau	GIA	st	Gelineau Gradual
Thine Honor Save, O Christ	Heermann, Loy	CON	s	The Lutheran Hymnal
This Day was Made By The Lord	C. Knoll/F. V. Strahan	HEL	s	The Catholic Liturgy Book
This Is The Day	Michael Joncas	WLP	s	Psalms For The Cantor,1
This Is The Day	Rory Cooney	NAL	ast	You Alone
This Is The Day	Michael Joncas	COO	ast	Every Stone Shall Cry
This Is The Day	Watts/Cruger	CON	s	The Lutheran Hymnal
This Is The Day	Christopher Willcock	PAA	ot	Psalms For Feasts & Seasons
This Is The Day	C. A. Peloquin	GIA	ao	Songs Of Israel
This Is The Day	James Marchionda	WLP	ast	Covenant
This Is The Day	John Foley	NAL	as	Wood Hath Hope
This Is The Day	J. Coller	OSB	s	Book Of Sacred Song
This Is The Day	John Lee	GIA		
This Is The Day	Lucien Deiss	WLP	s	Biblical Hymns & Psalms,2
This Is The Day	Lucien Deiss	WLP	s	People's Mass Book
This Is The Day	Proulx/Gelineau	GIA	o	
This Is The Day	Robert Twynham	PAA	o	Psalms & Acclamations
This Is The Day	Tim Schoenbachler	PAA	ast	All Is Ready
This Is The Day	Suzanne Toolan	RPB	st	Gather 'Round
This Is The Day	Robert E. Kreutz	GIA	s	ICEL Lectionary Music
This Is The Day	Angelo Della Picca	WLP	o	
This Is The Day	Gerard Farrell	OSB	o	
This Is The Day	M. Joncas	COO	as	Every Stone Shall Cry

119

Father Of Mercies	Steele/Wheall	CON	s	The Lutheran Hymnal
God's Word Is Our Great Heritage	Grundtvig/Luther	AUG	s	Lutheran Book Of Worship
Happy Are They	J. G. Phillips	WLP	s	Cantor Book
Happy Are They	William Callahan	ACP	s	Song Leader's Handbook
Happy Are They	P. Cunningham	GRA	ht	
Happy Are They	Anders	AUG	o	
Happy Are They	Batastini/Gelineau	GIA	st	Gelineau Gradual
How Blessed Are The Perfect	Westra/Bourgeois	HOP	s	The Service Hymnal
How Precious Is The Book	Fawcett/Walder	CON	s	The Lutheran Hymnal
How Shall The Young	Watts/Reinagle	CON	s	The Lutheran Hymnal
I Have Said	William Callahan	ACP	s	Song Leader's Handbook
Lamp Of Our Feet	Barton/Croft	CON	s	The Lutheran Hymnal
Let My Complaint Come	Adrian Batten	OXF	o	
Lord I Delight To Recall	Saward/Wilson	GIA	s	Psalm Praise
Lord I Love Your Commands	R. M. Hutmacher	GIA	o	
Lord I Love Your Commands	Batastini/Gelineau	GIA	st	Gelineau Gradual
Lord I Love Your Commands	E. Diemente	WLP	s	Cantor Book
Lord I Love Your Commands	P. Cunningham	GRA	ht	
Lord Jesus Christ My Savior	Hans C. Sthen	CON	s	The Lutheran Hymnal
Lord Jesus, Think On Me	Synesius Of Cyrene	CON	s	The Lutheran Hymnal
Lord Jesus, Think On Me	Synesius Of Cyrene	AUG	s	Lutheran Book Of Worship
Make Known Your Ways	Tim Schoenbachler	NAL	as	Songs For The Masses
My God Accept My Heart	Bridges/Este	CON	s	The Lutheran Hymnal
My Maker Be Thou Nigh	Rambach	CON	s	The Lutheran Hymnal
Not By Bread Alone	Donald J. Reagan	GIA	o	Celebration Series
O God Of Light	Taylor/Cabena	AUG	s	Lutheran Book Of Worship
O That The Lord Would Guide	Watts/Havergal	CON	s	The Lutheran Hymnal
O Word Of God Incarnate	William W. How	CON	s	The Lutheran Hymnal
O Word Of God Incarnate	William W. How	AUG	s	Lutheran Book Of Worship
Oh, That The Lord Would Guide	Watts/Havergal	AUG	s	Lutheran Book Of Worship
Teach Me O Lord	John Hilton	OXF	s	Two Psalms
Teach Me, O Lord	David Hurd	GIA	o	Choral Series,1985
The Will Of God	Dudley-Smith/Warren	GIA	s	Psalm Praise
They Are Happy	Richard Bewes	GIA	s	Psalm Praise
They Are Happy	Joseph Gelineau	GIA	s	20 Psalms & 3 Canticles
This Is The Day/psallite Deo	Jacques Berthier	GIA	as	Music From Taize,2
Thy Word Have I Hid	E. O. Sellers	HOP	s	Worship & Service Hymnal
Thy Word Is A Lamp To My Feet	Ernest O. Sellers	GPH	s	Hymns Of Glorious Praise
Your Word Is A Lamp	Eugene Englert	WLP	s	People's Mass Book,1984
Your Word Is A Lamp To My Feet	Joe Zsigray	NAL	as	Berakah

120
To The Lord In The Hour	Joseph Gelineau	GIA	s	24 Psalms & A Canticle

121
(With Wedding Responses)	William McKie	OXF	o	
Across The Sky	Hamilton/Decius	CON	s	The Lutheran Hymnal
Gracious Lord Again Is Ended	Neumann/Schop	CON	s	The Lutheran Hymnal
Hear Us, O Lord	Douglas Mews	GIA	s	ICEL Lectionary Music
I Lift My Eyes	S. Somerville	WLP	s	Psalms For Singing,Bk.2
I Lift My Eyes	Gregory Norbet	WES	ast	Winter's Coming Home
I Lift My Eyes	K. Jennings	AUG	o	
I Lift My Eyes	F. Hillebrand	AHC	ast	Long Way Home
I Lift My Eyes	Paul Wrynn	PAA	a	He Shall Be Peace
I Lift Up My Eyes	Michael Connolly	GIA	o	Choral Series,1985
I Lift Up My Eyes	Ray Repp	FEL	s	Hymnal For Young Christians
I Lift Up My Eyes	William Callahan	ACP	s	Song Leader's Handbook
I Lift Up My Eyes	Claude Goudimel	AUG	s	Psalms For The Church Year
I Lift Up My Eyes	Grail/C. Monaghan	RPB	amt	Modern Liturgy,9.8
I Lift Up My Eyes	Hal H. Hopson	GIA	o	
I Lift Up My Eyes	Joseph Gelineau	GIA	s	24 Psalms & A Canticle
I Love You, Lord, My Strength	Jeffrey Keyes	RPB	mt	Modern Liturgy,11.7
I To The Hills Will Lift	Scottish Psalter	PIL	s	Pilgrim Hymnal
I Will Lift Up Mine Eyes	Malcolm Williamson	BOH	s	Carols Of King David
I Will Lift Up Mine Eyes	John Rutter	OXF	o	
I Will Lift Up Mine Eyes	V. Eville	BOH		
I Will Lift Up Mine Eyes	Dudley-Smith/Baughen	GIA	s	Psalm Praise
I Will Lift Up Mine Eyes	John Gardner	OXF	o	
Let Us Go To God's House	Ralph Verdi	GIA	o	
Now The Hour Of Worship O'er	Schenck/Ahle	CON	s	The Lutheran Hymnal
Now The Shades Of Night	Occom/Knecht	CON	s	The Lutheran Hymnal
O God Be With Us	Herbert/Nigidius	CON	s	The Lutheran Hymnal
Oculi Nostri	Jacques Berthier	GIA	as	Music From Taize,2
Our Help Comes From The Lord	Howard Hughes	GIA	s	Praise God In Song
Our Help Comes From The Lord	Michael Joncas	GIA	s	Praise God In Song
Our Help Is From The Lord	David C. Isele	GIA	s	Praise God In Song
Our Help Is From The Lord	H. H. Smith	WLP	s	Cantor Book
Our Help Is From The Lord	John Foley	NAL	ast	Wood Hath Hope
Our Help Is From The Lord	Schiavone/Gelineau	GIA	st	Gelineau Gradual
Roll On Mighty Mountains	Paul Quinlan	NAL	a	Love And A Question
Sing Praise To God	Vulpius/Schutz	AUG	s	Lutheran Book Of Worship
Unto The Hills		MPH	s	The Book Of Hymns
Unto The Hills	Campbell/Purday	AUG	s	Lutheran Book Of Worship

122_____

Come, Let Us Go Rejoicing	Marty Haugen	GIA	s	Psalms For The Church Year
Give Peace O Lord	P. Cunningham	GRA	ht	
God Lord Of Sabaoth	Henry F. Chorley	CON	s	The Lutheran Hymnal
How I Rejoice	James Marchionda	WLP	ast	Covenant
How Happy I Was	S. Somerville	WLP	s	Psalms For Singing,Bk.2
I Rejoiced	Miriam Malone	RPB	st	Gather 'Round, Too
I Rejoiced	William Callahan	ACP	s	Song Leader's Handbook
I Rejoiced	B. Pulkingham	ERD	s	Sound Of Living Waters
I Rejoiced	Joseph Gelineau	GIA	s	24 Psalms & A Canticle
I Rejoiced	John Foley	NAL	as	Wood Hath Hope
I Rejoiced	John Foley	NAL	s	Glory And Praise,2
I Rejoiced	J. M. Burns	WLP	s	Cantor Book
I Rejoiced	Joseph Gelineau	GIA	s	Worship II
I Rejoiced When I Heard Them Say	Everett Frese	NPM	s	Advent Psalms
I Was Glad	Saward/Warren	GIA	s	Psalm Praise
I Was Glad	Peter Hallock	GIA	o	
I Was Glad	Roy Slack	OXF	o	
I Will Go Rejoicing	Donald J. Reagan	NPM	s	Mercy, Mercy
Let Us Go Rejoicing	Eugene E. Englert	WLP	s	Psalms For The Cantor,1
Let Us Go Rejoicing	David C. Isele	GIA	as	Songs Of David
Let Us Go Rejoicing	J. Coller	OSB	s	Book Of Sacred Song
Let Us Go Rejoicing	Kremer/Gelineau	GIA	st	Gelineau Gradual
Let Us Go Rejoicing	Christopher Willcock	PAA	ot	Psalms For Feasts & Seasons
O 'twas A Joyful Sound	Parker, Tate, Brady	CPF	s	The Hymnal 1940
O Jerusalem	M. Williamson	BOH		
What A Joy	Willard Jabusch	WLP	s	Hundredfold
With Glad Rejoicing	Jack Miffleton	WLP	ast	Drylands

123_____

I Lift My Eyes	Robert Kreutz	GIA	o	
Miserere Nobis	Jacques Berthier	GIA	as	Music From Taize,1
Our Eyes Are Fixed On The Lord	Angelo Della Picca	WLP	s	Cantor Book
Our Eyes Are Fixed On The Lord	Peloquin/Gelineau	GIA	st	Gelineau Gradual
To You I Have Lifted	Joseph Gelineau	GIA	s	24 Psalms & A Canticle
To You I Lift Up My Eyes	William Callahan	ACP	s	Song Leader's Handbook

124

As The Hills Are 'round Jerusalem	Helen Marie Gilsdorf	RPB	st	Gather 'Round
If God Had Not Been	Martin Luther	CON	s	The Lutheran Hymnal
If The Lord Had Not Been	Joseph Gelineau	GIA	s	30 Psalms & 2 Canticles
Where Would We All Be Now?	Michael Perry	GIA	s	Psalm Praise

125

Remember Your Mercies	Dorothy Mansheim	PAA	a	The Works Of God
They That Put Their Trust	Robin Orr	OXF	o	
They Who Trust In The Lord	Peter Hallick	GIA	o	
Those Who Put Their Trust	Joseph Gelineau	GIA	s	30 Psalms & 2 Canticles
Zion Stands By Hills	Kelly/Morely	CON	s	The Lutheran Hymnal

126

Psalm 126	Roger Sherman	GIA	o
Away They Went With Weeping	James Cavnar	WGM	as	Songs Of Praise.1
Long Way Home	F. Hillebrand	AHC	ast	Long Way Home
May The Lord Bless Us	P. Cunningham	GRA	ht
Oh That I Had 1000 Voices	Mentzer/Konig	AUG	s	Lutheran Book Of Worship
Oh That I Had 1000 Voices	Mentzer/Konig	CON	s	The Lutheran Hymnal
Redemption From Captivity	H. B. Hays	OSB	s	Benedictine Book Of Song
Son Of David	John Foley	NAL	s	Glory And Praise.2
The Lord Has Done Great Deeds	Tim Schoenbachler	NAL	as	O Jerusalem
The Lord Has Done Great Things	Everett Frese	NPM	s	Advent Psalms
The Lord Has Done Great Things	J. G. Phillips	WLP	s	Cantor Book
The Lord Has Done Great Things	Michael Lynch	RAV	as	With All My Heart
The Lord Has Done Great Things	Proulx/Gelineau	GIA	st	Gelineau Gradual
The Lord Has Done Great Things	P. Cunningham	GRA	ht
The Lord Has Done Great Things	Robert Twynham	GIA	o
The Lord Has Done Great Things	"Eleven: fifty-nine"	ERD	s	Sound Of Living Waters
These Are They	Mary Grace Zunic	FEL	s	Hymnal For Young Christians
What Great Marvels	Helen Marie Gilsdorf	RPB	st	Gather 'Round
When God Delivered Israel	Saward/Warren	GIA	s	Psalm Praise
When From Our Exile	Oosterhuis/Huijbers	NAL	as	When From Our Exile
When The Lord Brought	William Callahan	ACP	s	Song Leader's Handbook
When The Lord Turned	Joseph Gelineau	GIA	s	24 Psalms & A Canticle

127

If The Building Is Not	David Wilson	GIA	s	Psalm Praise
If The Lord Does Not Build	Dan Schutte	NAL	as	Earthen Vessels
If The Lord Does Not Build	Joseph Gelineau	GIA	s	24 Psalms & A Canticle
O Father All Creating	John Ellerton	CON	s	The Lutheran Hymnal
Poor Builder	F. Hillebrand	AHC	ast	Long Way Home
Unless The Lord	Westendorf/Picca	WLP	s	People's Mass Book

128

A Wedding Song	Robert Wetzler	AUG	o	
Blessed Are Those	Grail/Downey Et Al.	RPB	amt	Modern Liturgy,9.8
Blessed Is Everyone	M. Praetorius	AUG	s	Psalms For The Church Year
Blessing For The Devout	Larry Florian	PAA	a	More Than The Sands
Blest Are Those	Ken Meltz	WLP		1981
Happy Are Those	Bill Foster	RPB	at	If I Forget You, Jerusalem
Happy Are Those	Bill Foster	RPB	m	Modern Liturgy,10.2
Happy Are Those	J. G. Phillips	WLP	s	Cantor Book
Happy Are Those	J. M. Burns	WLP	s	Cantor Book
Happy Are Those	Murray/Gelineau	GIA	st	Gelineau Gradual
Happy Are You	William Callahan	ACP	s	Song Leader's Handbook
Happy Is The Man	Oosterhuis/Huijbers	NAL	as	When From Our Exile
How Happy Are You	mer Westendorf	WLP	s	People's Mass Book,1984
How Happy You Who Fear	S. Somerville	WLP	s	Psalms For Singing,Bk.2
How Happy You	Westendorf/Dean	WLP	s	People's Mass Book
Keep Alive	F. Hillebrand	AHC	ast	Long Way Home
Like Olive Branches	Lucien Deiss	WLP	s	People's Mass Book
May The Lord Bless Us	Angelo Della Picca	WLP	s	Cantor Book
May The Lord Bless Us	Carroll/Gelineau	GIA	st	Gelineau Gradual
May You See Your Children's	D. Fitzpatrick	FEL		
O Blessed Are Those	Joseph Gelineau	GIA	s	24 Psalms & A Canticle
O Blessed Are Those	Joseph Gelineau	GIA	s	Worship II
O Blessed Home	Landstad	CON	s	The Lutheran Hymnal
The Lord Is Near	Douglas Mews	GIA	s	ICEL Lectionary Music
We Praise You	Balhoff/Ducote Et Al.	NAL	as	Remember Your Love
We Praise You	Balhoff/Ducote Et Al.	NAL	s	Glory And Praise,2
Your Wife Shall Be	Judy O'Sheil	FEL	s	Hymnal For Young Christians
Your Wife Shall Be	P. Cunningham	GRA	ht	

129

Rescue Me From My Enemies	John Foley	NAL	as	Neither Silver Nor Gold
They Have Pressed Me Hard	Joseph Gelineau	GIA	s	Grail-Gelineau Psalter

130

Psalm 130	Richard Proulx	GIA	o	
Psalm 130	Schutz/Reuning	GIA	s	The Becker Psalter
De Profundis	C. A. Peloquin	GIA	ao	An American Liturgy
Domine Deus	Jacques Berthier	GIA	as	Music From Taize,2
From Depths Of Woe	Martin Luther	CON	s	The Lutheran Hymnal
From The Deep	Luke Connaughton	HEL	s	The Catholic Liturgy Book
From The Depths	Lucien Deiss	WLP		
From The Depths	Michael Gilligan	ACP		
From The Depths	Paul Quinlan	FEL	s	Hymnal For Young Christians
From The Depths	Willard Jabusch	FEL	s	Hymnal For Young Christians
From The Depths	Willard Jabusch	WLP	as	Enter In The Wilderness
From The Depths	Barnes/Wilson	GIA	s	Psalm Praise
Hear Us O Lord	Balhoff/Ducote Et Al.	NAL	as	Remember Your Love
Hear Us, Lord, And Save Us	G. Farrell	OSB	s	Book Of Sacred Song
I Cry To You	Marivoet/de Vocht	HEL	s	The Catholic Liturgy Book
I Wait For God	Gregory Norbet	WES	ast	So Full Of Deep Joy
Kindness	Jack Miffleton	WLP	ast	Drylands
Kindness	Jack Miffleton	WLP	s	People's Mass Book,1984
Lord, From The Depths	Lucien Deiss	WLP	s	People's Mass Book,1984
My Soul, My Soul Hopes In The Lo	Ralph Hooper	GIA	s	ICEL Lectionary Music
Out Of The Deep	M. Williamson	BOH		
Out Of The Deep	Baker/Daman	CON	s	The Lutheran Hymnal
Out Of The Deep	John Alcock	PRE	o	
Out Of The Depths	D. Fitzpatrick	FEL		
Out Of The Depths	E. Englert	WLP	o	
Out Of The Depths	H. B. Hays	OSB	s	Benedictine Book Of Song
Out Of The Depths	J. Chepponis	GIA	o	
Out Of The Depths	J. Cunningham/M.QuinnWLP		s	People's Mass Book
Out Of The Depths	Joseph Gelineau	GIA	s	24 Psalms & A Canticle
Out Of The Depths	Joseph Gelineau	GIA	s	Worship II
Out Of The Depths	M. Praetorius	AUG	s	Psalms For The Church Year
Out Of The Depths	Martin Luther	AUG	s	Lutheran Book Of Worship
Out Of The Depths	S. Somerville	WLP	s	Psalms For Singing,Bk.1
Out Of The Depths	William Callahan	ACP	s	Song Leader's Handbook
Out Of The Depths	Winkworth/Luther	MPH	s	The Book Of Hymns
Out Of The Depths		ACP	s	The Johannine Hymnal
Out Of The Depths	Alan Hovhaness	CFP		
Remember Your Love	Balhoff/Ducote Et Al.	NAL	as	Remember Your Love
Remember Your Love	Balhoff/Ducote Et Al.	NAL	s	Glory And Praise,2
Remember, O Lord	Christopher Willcock	GIA	s	ICEL Lectionary Music
Teach Us	Steven Farney		mt	Modern Liturgy,12.6
Turn To Me, Lord	Tim Schoenbachler	NAL	ast	O Jerusalem
With The Lord There Is Mercy	Muriel Hurtel	WLP	s	Psalms For The Cantor,1
With The Lord There Is Mercy	Marty Haugen	GIA	s	Psalms For The Church Year
With The Lord There Is Mercy	Christopher Willcock	PAA	ot	Psalms For Feasts & Seasons
With The Lord There Is Mercy	Ralph Hooper	GIA	s	ICEL Lectionary Music
With The Lord There Is Mercy	W. A. Jurgens	OSB	s	Book Of Sacred Song
With The Lord There Is Mercy	C. Knoll/F.V.Strahan	HEL	s	The Catholic Liturgy Book
With The Lord There Is Mercy	Angelo Della Picca	WLP	o	
With The Lord There Is Mercy	Carroll/Gelineau	GIA	st	Gelineau Gradual

131

Psalm 131	Jack Beeson	OXF s	The Bay Psalm Book
As A Little Child	Helen Marie Gilsdorf	RPB at	In The Breaking Of Bread
As A Little Child	Helen Marie Gilsdorf	RPB m	Modern Liturgy,8.5
Calm And Quiet	Ron Walters	RPB mt	Modern Liturgy,5.3
Come To The Quiet	John M. Talbot	CLM ast	Come To The Quiet
Enormous Dreams	F. Hillebrand	AHC ast	Long Way Home
Enough For Me	Larry Folk	NAL ast	Living Jesus
In The Lord I Find Peace	P. Cunningham	GRA ht	
In You, Lord, I Have Found	Batastini/Gelineau	GIA st	Gelineau Gradual
In You, Lord, I Have Found	E. Diemente	WLP s	Cantor Book
In You, O Lord	Robert Ellis	NPM s	Appalachian Folk Hymn Mass
Israel, Rely On Yahweh	Mike Fitzgerald	WGM as	Songs Of Praise,1
Like A Child	Jerry Liberstein	FEL s	Hymnal For Young Christians
Lord Forever At Thy Side	Montgomery/Gibbons	CPF s	The Hymnal 1940
Lord, Forever At Your Side	Montgomery/Shaw	HEL s	The Catholic Liturgy Book
Lord, Go Up To The Place	Hughes/Gelineau	GIA st	Gelineau Gradual
My Soul Is Longing	Lucien Deiss	WLP s	Biblical Hymns & Psalms,1
My Soul Is Longing	Lucien Deiss	WLP s	People's Mass Book
My Soul Is Longing	Lucien Deiss	WLP s	People's Mass Book,1984
My Soul Is Longing	Lucien Deiss	WLP a	Like Olive Branches
O Lord, My Heart	William Callahan	ACP s	Song Leader's Handbook
O Lord, My Heart Is Not Proud	Joseph Gelineau	GIA s	30 Psalms & 2 Canticles
Peace	Dorothy Mansheim	PAA a	The Works Of God
Peace Of Jerusalem	Dave Brubeck	SFM o	Mass - To Hope

132

O Lord, Remember David	Joseph Gelineau	GIA s	Grail-Gelineau Psalter
Pour Out Thy Spirit	J. Montgomery	CON s	The Lutheran Hymnal

133

Behold How Good	K. Thomerson	ERD	s	Sound Of Living Waters
Behold How Good	Stanley Vann	OXF	o	
Behold How Good	C. A. Peloquin	GIA	o	
Behold How Good	D. Pinkham	CFP	o	
How Good A Thing It Is	Seddon/Warren	GIA	s	Psalm Praise
How Good And How Pleasant	Joseph Gelineau	GIA	s	Grail-Gelineau Psalter
How Good And How Pleasant	Tobias Colgan	ABB	ast	Songs Like Incense
Oh, How Good	Carey Landry	NAL	st	Glory And Praise,1
Oh, How Good	Carey Landry	NAL	as	Abba, Father
See How Good It Is	S. Somerville	WLP	s	Psalms For Singing,Bk.2

134

Psalm 134	Ned Rorem	SOM	s	Two Holy Songs
Behold Now, Bless The Lord	Richard Proulx	GIA	o	
Come And Praise The Lord	Randall DeBruyn	OCP	s	Choral Praise — 1985
Come Sing The Blessings	S. Somerville	WLP	s	Psalms For Singing,Bk.1
In The Silent Hours Of Night	Howard Hughes	GIA	s	Praise God In Song
Into Your Hands	Lucien Deiss	WLP	s	Sing For The Lord
Into Your Hands	Lucien Deiss	WLP	at	Let The Earth Shout
Lift Up Your Hands	Harold Owen	GIA	o	Choral Series,1985
O Come Bless The Lord	Joseph Gelineau	IA	s	30 Psalms & 2 Canticles

135

Father Of Glory	Watts/Cruger	CON	s	The Lutheran Hymnal
I Have Learned	Larry Florian	PAA	as	More Than The Sands
Praise The Name Of The Lord	Joseph Gelineau	GIA	s	Grail-Gelineau Psalter
Sing To His Name	Jane Marshall	GIA	o	Choral Series,1985
To Our Redeemer's Glorious Name	Steele/Wheall	CON	s	The Lutheran Hymnal
We Praise You	Balhoff/Ducote Et Al.	NAL	s	Glory And Praise,2
We Praise You	Balhoff/Ducote Et Al.	NAL	as	Remember Your Love
You Servants Of God	Wesley/J. M. Haydn	AUG	s	Lutheran Book Of Worship

136

A Children's Thanksgiving	P. Cunningham	RPB	mt	Modern Liturgy,5.4
Alleluia	John Lee	OSB	s	Book Of Sacred Song
Dayenu		ACP	s	The Johannine Hymnal
Eternal Is His Mercy	Michael Joncas	NAL	ast	On Eagle's Wings
Faith, Hope And Love	C. A. Peloquin	GIA	ao	Lyric Liturgy
For His Love Endures Forever	Rick Bennett	RPB	mt	Modern Liturgy,5.2
Give Thanks To The Lord	Westendorf/Takacs	WLP	s	People's Mass Book
Give Thanks To The Lord	C. A. Peloquin	GIA	ao	Songs Of Israel
Give Thanks To The Lord	William Callahan	ACP	s	Song Leader's Handbook
Give Thanks Unto The Lord	Robert Starer	SOM	o	
Give To Our God	Watts/Hatton	AUG	s	Lutheran Book Of Worship
His Love Is Everlasting	Angelo Della Picca	WLP	s	Psalms For The Cantor,1
His Love Is Everlasting	D. Haas & M. Haugen	GIA	s	Psalms For The Church Year
His Love Is Everlasting	Christopher Willcock	PAA	ot	Psalms For Feasts & Seasons
His Love Is Everlasting	G. Farrell	OSB	s	Book Of Sacred Song
His Love Is Lasting	F. Hillebrand	AHC	ast	Long Way Home
His Mercy Endures Forever	Jeffrey Keyes	RPB	mt	Modern Liturgy, 6.4
Let Us With A Gladsome Mind	Milton/Monk	MPH	s	The Book Of Hymns
Let Us With A Gladsome Mind	Milton/Moe	AUG	s	Lutheran Book Of Worship
Let Us With A Gladsome Mind	Milton, Wilkes	CPF	s	The Hymnal 1940
Let Us With A Gladsome Mind	John Milton	PIL	s	Pilgrim Hymnal
Let Us With A Gladsome Mind	John Milton	HEL	s	The Catholic Liturgy Book
Mountains And Hills	Dan Schutte	NAL	as	Neither Silver Nor Gold
Mountains And Hills	Dan Schutte	NAL	s	Glory And Praise,2
O Give Thanks To The Lord	Joseph Gelineau	GIA	s	24 Psalms & A Canticle
O Thank The Lord	Dudley-Smith/Baughen	GIA	s	Psalm Praise
Praise God	Dufford, Foley	NAL	as	A Dwelling Place

Praise God, Praise Him Here	Paul Quinlan	FEL	s	Hymnal For Young Christians
Praise Oh Praise Our God	Milton, Baker	CON	s	The Lutheran Hymnal
The Reproaches	William Shafer	ACP	s	The Johannine Hymnal
We Praise You	Balhoff/Ducote Et Al.	NAL	s	Glory And Praise,2
We Praise You	Balhoff/Ducote Et Al.	NAL	as	Remember Your Love

137

Babylon	Tim Schoenbachler	PAA	ast	All Is Ready
By Flowing Waters Of Babylon	Michael Perry	GIA	s	Psalm Praise
By Streams Of Babylon	Willard Jabusch	FEL	s	Hymnal For Young Christians
By The Babylonian Rivers	Ewald Bash	MPH	s	Suppl. To Book Of Hymns
By The Rivers Of Babylon	Joseph Gelineau	GIA	s	30 Psalms & 2 Canticles
By The Rivers Of Babylon	D. Fitzpatrick	FEL		
By The Streams Of Babylon	William Callahan	ACP	s	Song Leader's Handbook
By The Streams Of Babylon	Bob Hurd	FEL		
By The Streams Of Babylon	Howard Hughes	WLP		
By The Streams Of Babylon	P. Cunningham	GIA	o	
By The Waters Of Babylon	Colin Mawby	GIA	s	Four Psalm Settings
I Love Thy Kingdom	Dwight/Williams	CON	s	The Lutheran Hymnal
I Love Your Kingdom	Dwight/Williams	AUG	s	Lutheran Book Of Worship
Let My Tongue Be Silenced	P. Cunningham	GRA	ht	
Let My Tongue Be Silenced	Ron Ellis	RAV		
Let My Tongue Be Silent	Howard Hughes	WLP	s	Cantor Book
Let My Tongue Be Silent	Schiavone/Gelineau	GIA	st	Gelineau Gradual
O God Our Help In Ages Past	A. Hovhaness	CFP		
Rivers Of Babylon	Gregory Norbet	WES	as	Calm Is The Night
Streams Of Babylon	F. Hillebrand	AHC	ast	Long Way Home

138

An Everlasting Song	Phillip D. Sessions	RPB	mt	Modern Liturgy,11.5
Deep From My Heart	Paul Quinlan	NAL	a	Love And A Question
Great Is The Glory Of The Lord	Cheline/Baxter	OCP	s	Choral Praise — 1985
I Thank You Lord	Joseph Gelineau	GIA	s	30 Psalms & 2 Canticles
I Thank You Lord	Michael Baughen	GIA	s	Psalm Praise
I Will Give Thanks	Angel Tucciarone	RPB	st	Gather 'Round, Too
I Will Give Thanks	William Callahan	ACP	s	Song Leader's Handbook
I Will Give Thanks	Angelo Della Picca	WLP	s	Cantor Book
In The Sight Of The Angels	J. G. Phillips	WLP	s	Cantor Book
In The Sight Of The Angels	Carroll/Gelineau	GIA	st	Gelineau Gradual
Lord, I Thank You	Angelo Della Picca	WLP	s	Cantor Book
Lord, On The Day I Called	Proulx/Gelineau	GIA	st	Gelineau Gradual
Lord, On The Day I Called	M. Fautch	WLP	s	Cantor Book
Lord, Your Love Is Eternal	R. J. Schaffer	WLP	st	Cantor Book
Lord, Your Love Is Eternal	Bill Foster	RPB	m	Modern Liturgy,10.2
Lord, Your Love Is Eternal	Bill Foster	RPB	at	If I Forget You, Jerusalem
Lord, Your Love Is Eternal	Proulx/Gelineau	GIA	st	Gelineau Gradual
We Give Thanks	Larry Folk	NAL	ast	Living Jesus
When I Had Fallen		ACP	s	The Johannine Hymnal

139

Draw Me To You	James Marchionda	WLP	ast	Covenant
Guide Me Lord	Howard Hughes	GIA	o	
I Praise You	Batastini/Gelineau	GIA	st	Gelineau Gradual
I Praise You	Robert Kreutz	WLP	s	Cantor Book
If I Take The Wings Of Morning	Peggy Beaudoin	RPB	mt	Modern Liturgy,6.1
Lord To Thee I Make Confession	Frank/Cruger	CON	s	The Lutheran Hymnal
Lord You've Tested Me	Saward/Jacob	GIA	s	Psalm Praise
Lord You've Tested Me	Saward/Warren	GIA	s	Psalm Praise
Lord, You Have Known Me	Jeanette Goglia	RPB	m	Modern Liturgy,10.6
Lord, You Have Probed Me	Helen Marie Gilsdorf	RPB	mt	Modern Liturgy,6.3
Lord, You Probed Me	Mischke/Lindusky	WLP	s	People's Mass Book,1984
Now Rest Beneath Night's Shadow	Gerhardt/Isaak	CON	s	The Lutheran Hymnal
Now That The Day	Hertzog/Krieger	CON	s	The Lutheran Hymnal
O Lord You Search Me	Joseph Gelineau	GIA	s	30 Psalms & 2 Canticles
Still, Still With Thee	Harriet B. Stowe	MPH	s	The Book Of Hymns

Stilled And Quiet Is My Soul	Suzanne Toolan	GIA	ao	Living Spirit
The Lord Is My Light	Peter Hallock	GIA	o	St. Mark's Cathedral Series
The Hound Of Heaven	Christopher Willcock	PAA	st	Let All The Peoples

140

Redeemer King		ACP	s	The Johannine Hymnal
Rescue Me, Lord	Joseph Gelineau	GIA	s	Grail-Gelineau Psalter

141

Be Gracious, O Lord	John Allyn Melloh	GIA	s	Praise God In Song
How Blessed Is This Place	E. E. Ryden	AUG	s	Lutheran Book Of Worship
I Have Called To You Lord	Joseph Gelineau	GIA	s	Grail-Gelineau Psalter
I Have Called To You Lord	Joseph Gelineau	GIA	s	Worship II
Into Your Hands	Lucien Deiss	WLP	at	Let The Earth Shout
Into Your Hands	Lucien Deiss	WLP	s	Sing For The Lord
Let My Prayer Rise	Darryl Ducote	NAL	ast	Morning To Night
Let My Prayer Rise	Howard Hughes	GIA	s	Praise God In Song
Let My Prayer Rise	C.Knoll/F.V.Strahan	HEL	s	The Catholic Liturgy Book
Like Burning Incense	Michael Joncas	NAL	ast	O Joyful Light
My Prayers Come Before You	Tobias Colgan	ABB	ast	Songs Like Incense
My Prayers Rise Like Incense	Howard Hughes	GIA	s	Praise God In Song
My Prayers Rise Like Incense	Ken Meltz	WLP	s	People's Mass Book,1984
My Prayers Rise Like Incense	Michael Joncas	GIA	s	Praise God In Song
My Prayers Rise Like Incense	Robert Twynham	PAA	o	Psalms & Acclamations
My Prayers Rise Like Incense	David C. Isele	GIA	s	Praise God In Song
Round Me Falls The Night	Romanis/Drese	CON	s	The Lutheran Hymnal
Softly Now The Light Of Day	Doane/Gottschalk	MPH	s	The Book Of Hymns

142

Psalm 142	Ned Rorem	SOM	s	Cycle Of Holy Songs
God Forbid	William Shafer	ACP	s	The Johannine Hymnal
Lord, You Are My Refuge	C.Knoll/F.V.Strahan	HEL	s	The Catholic Liturgy Book
With All My Voice	Joseph Gelineau	GIA	s	Grail-Gelineau Psalter

143

Psalm 143	Schutz/Reuning	GIA	s	The Becker Psalter
And Wilt Thou Pardon	Joseph The Hymngrphr	CON	s	The Lutheran Hymnal
Lord, Listen To My Prayer	Joseph Gelineau	GIA	s	Grail-Gelineau Psalter
My God, My Father	Mann/Meyer	CON	s	The Lutheran Hymnal

144

| Blessed Be The Lord | Joseph Gelineau | GIA | s | Grail-Gelineau Psalter |
| David's House | M. Williamson | BOH | | |

145

All Creatures Of Our God	Francis Of Assisi	AUG	s	Lutheran Book Of Worship
All Thy Works Shall Praise	William Mathias	OXF	o	
Before The Lord We Bow	Key/Darwall	CON	s	The Lutheran Hymnal
Before You, Lord, We Bow	Key/Darwall	AUG	s	Lutheran Book Of Worship
Every Day	William Callahan	ACP	s	Song Leader's Handbook
Every Day I Will Praise You	Helen Marie Gilsdorf	RPB	st	Gather 'Round, Too
Feed Thy Children	Heerman/Cruger	CON	s	The Lutheran Hymnal
Glory I Will Give	William Callahan	ACP	s	Song Leader's Handbook
God My King Thy Might Confer	Mant, Witt	CPF	s	The Hymnal 1940
I Will Exalt You	Peter Hallock	GIA	o	
I Will Extol Thee	S. P. Folkemer	GIA	o	
I Will Extol You	William Callahan	ACP	s	Song Leader's Handbook
I Will Extol You	Charles Christmas	WGM	as	Songs Of Praise,1
I Will Give You Glory	Joseph Gelineau	GIA	s	30 Psalms & 2 Canticles
I Will Praise Your Name	David Haas	GIA	s	Psalms For The Church Year
I Will Praise Your Name	Howard L. Hughes	WLP	s	Psalms For The Cantor,1
I Will Praise Your Name	Christopher Willcock	PAA	ot	Psalms For Feasts & Seasons
I Will Praise Your Name	W. A. Jurgens	OSB	s	Book Of Sacred Song
I Will Praise Your Name	Carroll/Gelineau	GIA	st	Gelineau Gradual
I Will Proclaim You	S. Somerville	WLP	s	Psalms For Singing,Bk.1
Keeping Festival	Suzanne Toolan	RPB	ast	Keeping Festival
Let All Your Works	William Callahan	ACP	s	Song Leader's Handbook
Praise God	Gary Ault	NAL	ast	Beginning Today
Praise God	Gary Ault	HEL	s	The Catholic Liturgy Book
Praise The Lord	William Callahan	ACP	s	Song Leader's Handbook
Psalm Of Thanksgiving	Harold Darke	OXF	o	
The Lord Is Compassionate	Larry Folk	NAL	ast	Living Jesus
The Lord Is Gracious	William Callahan	ACP	s	Song Leader's Handbook
The Lord Is Near	E. Diemente	WLP	s	Cantor Book
The Lord Is Near	Schiavone/Gelineau	GIA	st	Gelineau Gradual
The Lord Is Near	Jeffrey Hamm	PAA	a	The Works Of God
The Lord Is Near	David C. Isele	GIA	s	Praise God In Song
The Eyes Of All Wait Upon Thee	Robert E. Smith	BBL	o	
The Hand Of The Lord	Angelo Della Picca	WLP	s	Cantor Book
The Hand Of The Lord	Dorothy Mansheim	PAA	a	The Works Of God
The Hand Of The Lord	Kelly/Gelineau	GIA	st	Gelineau Gradual
The Sun Arises Now	Kingo, Paulsen/Zinck	CON	s	The Lutheran Hymnal
We Praise You, O Lord	Christopher Willcock	GIA	s	ICEL Lectionary Music

146

Psalm 146	Harold Shapero	SOM	s	Two Psalms
Psalm 146	Robert Powell	GIA	o	
A Song To The Lord	James Marchionda	WLP	ast	Covenant
All My Life	Bob Hurd	PAA	ast	Roll Down The Ages
Happy The Poor In Spirit	Peloquin/Gelineau	GIA	st	Gelineau Gradual
Happy The Poor In Spirit	J. M. Burns	WLP	s	Cantor Book
I Will Praise The Lord	David C. Isele	GIA	s	Praise God In Song
I Will Praise The Lord	C. Knoll/F.V.Strahan	HEL	s	The Catholic Liturgy Book
I'll Praise My Maker	Watts/Ripper	ABI	o	
I'll Praise My Maker	Isaac Watts	MPH	s	The Book Of Hymns
If Anyone Serves Me	Robert Kreutz	ICE²	s	Music For The Rites
Keeping Festival	Suzanne Toolan	RPB	ast	Keeping Festival
Lord Come And Save Us	Michael Joncas	NAL	ast	On Eagle's Wings
Lord Come And Save Us	Batastini/Gelineau	GIA	st	Gelineau Gradual
Lord Come And Save Us	H. H. Smith	WLP	s	Cantor Book
Lord Come And Save Us	Joseph Gelineau	GIA	st	Gelineau Gradual
Lord, Come And Save Us	Everett Frese	NPM	s	Advent Psalms
My Soul Sing	Barnes/Wilson	GIA	s	Psalm Praise
Praise The Lord For He Is Good	Christopher Willcock	GIA	s	ICEL Lectionary Music
Praise The Lord My Soul	Proulx/Gelineau	GIA	st	Gelineau Gradual
Praise The Lord My Soul	P. Cunningham	GRA	ht	
Praise The Lord My Soul	E. Diemente	WLP	s	Cantor Book
Praise The Almighty	Herrnschmidt	AUG	s	Lutheran Book Of Worship
Praise The Almighty My Soul	Alfred Brauer	CON	s	The Lutheran Hymnal
Praise Thou The Lord O My Soul	Pfatteicher	PIL	s	Pilgrim Hymnal
The God Of Jacob	William Callahan	ACP	s	Song Leader's Handbook
The Lord God	William Callahan	ACP	s	Song Leader's Handbook
The Lord Keeps Faith	William Callahan	ACP	s	Song Leader's Handbook

147

Fill Your Hearts	Dudley Smith/Coulthar	GIA	s	Psalm Praise
From All Who Dwell	Louis Bourgeois	ACP	s	The Johannine Hymnal
Glorify The Lord	William Callahan	ACP	s	Song Leader's Handbook
He Heals The Broken Hearted	P. Cunningham	GRA	ht	
Keeping Festival	Suzanne Toolan	RPB	ast	Keeping Festival
Praise God For He Is Good	Joseph Gelineau	GIA	s	20 Psalms & 3 Canticles
Praise The Lord	William Callahan	ACP	s	Song Leader's Handbook
Praise The Lord O Jerusalem	M. Williamson	BOH		
Praise The Lord Who Heals	Batastini/Gelineau	GIA	st	Gelineau Gradual
Praise The Lord Who Heals	Howard Hughes	WLP	s	Cantor Book
Praise The Lord Who Heals	Michael Lynch	RAV		
Praise The Lord, Jerusalem	J. M. Burns	WLP	s	Cantor Book
Praise The Lord, Jerusalem	Kreutz/Gelineau	GIA	st	Gelineau Gradual
Rejoice Ye Pure In Heart	Plumtre/Messiter	MPH	s	The Book Of Hymns
The Word Of God Became Man	Proulx/Gelineau	GIA	st	Gelineau Gradual
The Word Of God Became Man	J. G. Phillips	GIA	st	Gelineau Gradual
This Is The Day	C. A. Peloquin	GIA	o	
This Is The Day	Lucien Deiss	WLP		
This Is The Day	Suzanne Toolan	RPB	st	Gather 'Round

148

Psalm 148	Joseph Gelineau	GIA	s	20 Psalms & 3 Canticles
Psalm 148	J. Hamm & D.Mansheim	PAA	ast	The Works Of God
Psalm 148	Ned Rorem	SOM	s	Cycle Of Holy Songs
All Creatures Of Our God	Francis Of Assisi	AUG	s	Lutheran Book Of Worship
Alleluia Praise The Lord	Robert Kreutz	GIA	o	
Angels All Around Him	William Callahan	ACP	s	Song Leader's Handbook
Canticle Of The 3 Young Men		WGM	as	Songs Of Praise,1
From 'Come Follow'	Jerry Kramper	GIA	o	
From All Who Dwell	Louis Bourgeois	ACP	s	The Johannine Hymnal
Glory, Praise To You	Lucien Deiss	NAL	ast	Awaken, My Heart
Grant To Me, Lord	Jeffrey Keyes	RPB	mt	Modern Liturgy,5.6
Heaven And Earth Are Filled	Howard Hughes	GIA	o	
Holy, Holy, Holy	Tobias Colgan	ABB	ast	Songs Like Incense
In Praise Of His Name	Roc O'Connor	NAL	st	Glory And Praise,1
In Praise Of His Name	Roc O'Connor	NAL	as	A Dwelling Place
Jesus Is Life	Carey Landry	NAL	st	Glory And Praise,1
Jesus Is Life	Carey Landry	NAL	as	Abba, Father
Let The Whole Creation Cry	Brooke/Anton	AUG	s	Lutheran Book Of Worship
Melismatic	Alan Hovhaness	CFP		
Mighty Lord	John Foley	NAL	st	Glory And Praise,2
Mighty Lord	John Foley	NAL	as	Wood Hath Hope
O Praise The Lord Of Heaven	Colin Mawby	GIA	s	Four Psalm Settings

Oh That I Had 1000 Voices	Mentzer/Dretzel	CON	s	The Lutheran Hymnal
Praise Him	Perry/Warren	GIA	s	Worship II
Praise Him	Perry/Coates	GIA	s	Psalm Praise
Praise Him	Perry/Warren	GIA	s	Psalm Praise
Praise The Lord	Thomas Browne	ACP	s	The Johannine Hymnal
Praise The Lord	Kelly/Colgan	OSB	s	Benedictine Book Of Song
Praise The Lord O Heavens	anon/F. J. Haydn	AUG	s	Lutheran Book Of Worship
Praise The Lord O Heavens	Osler/Pritchard	WLP	s	People's Mass Book
Praise The Lord From The Heavens	Howard Hughes	GIA	s	Paise God In Song
Praise The Lord Of Heaven	Thomas Browne	WLP	s	People's Mass Book
Praise The Lord Of Heaven	Dudley-Smith/Warren	GIA	s	Psalm Praise
Praise The Lord Of Heaven	T. Browne/French Noel	HEL	s	The Catholic Liturgy Book
Praise The Lord Of Heaven	Thomas Browne	AUG	s	Lutheran Book Of Worship
Praise The Lord Our God	Bewes/Wilson	GIA	s	Psalm Praise
Praise The Lord Ye Heavens	Prichard	PIL	s	Pilgrim Hymnal
Praise The Lord, Ye Heavens	J. Willcox	HOP	s	Worship & Service Hymnal
Praise The Lord, You Heavens	Osler/Prichard	HEL	s	The Catholic Liturgy Book
Sing To The Lord	Balhoff/Ducote Et Al.	NAL	as	Remember Your Love
Sing To The Lord	Balhoff/Ducote Et Al.	NAL	s	Glory And Praise,2
The Lord Jehovah Reigns	Watts/Millenium	MPH	s	The Book Of Hymns
The Word Of God	J. G. Phillips	WLP	s	Cantor Book
When We Pray	Jack Miffleton	WLP	ast	Holy House
Ye Watchers And Ye Holy Ones	John A. Riley	CON	s	The Lutheran Hymnal
Ye Watchers And Ye Holy Ones	John A. Riley	AUG	s	Lutheran Book Of Worship

149

Psalm 149	Carol Dick	PAA	aos	In The Land Of The Living
Jesus Is Life	Carey Landry	NAL	as	Abba, Father
Jesus Is Life	Carey Landry	NAL	st	Glory And Praise,1
Praise The Lord From Heaven	Joseph Gelineau	GIA		
Sing A New Song	Joseph Gelineau	GIA	s	Grail-Gelineau Psalter
Sing A New Song	Seddon/Warren	GIA	s	Psalm Praise
Sing To God A Brand New Canticle	Paul Quinlan	NAL	s	Glory And Praise,2
Sing To God A Brand New Canticle	Paul Quinlan	NAL	as	Songs Of Praise,1
We Sing The Almighty Power	Isaac Watts	CON	s	The Lutheran Hymnal

Psalm 150

To You,
to You above,
to You above holy
and strong,
be joy,
be joy from us
for boundless lifegiving
power,
joy from
our trumpets, joy
from our lyrical strings,
joy from
our drums
and dances and
harps, pipes, and shivering
cymbals,
joy from
our clashing, our
ringing with all that lives
to You!

Francis Patrick Sullivan
©1983 National Association of Pastoral Musicians

150

Psalm 150	Barrie Cabena	OXF		
Psalm 150	Don McAfee	SOM	o	
Psalm 150	Jack C. Goode	ABI		
Psalm 150	John Harper	OXF	o	
Psalm 150	Lewandowski	FLA	o	
Psalm 150	Ned Rorem	SOM	s	Two Holy Songs
Psalm 150	Pfautsch	FLA	o	
Psalm 150	Schutz/Reuning	GIA	s	Becker Psalter
Psalm 150	William Mathias	OXF	o	
Psalm 150	Zoltan Kodaly	OXF		
Alleluia, Praise The Lord!	Wesley/Lovelace	WRD	s	Cathedral Praise
Alleluia, Praise To You	Lucien Deiss	WLP		
Bless'd Be The Lord Our God	Howard Hughes	GIA	s	Praise God In Song
Blest Be The Lord In Song	David C. Isele	GIA	s	Praise God In Song
Blest Be The Lord Our God	Michael Joncas	GIA	s	Praise God In Song
Come To The Lord	Helen Marie Gilsdorf	RPB	st	Gather 'Round
Glory To God	Saward/Warren	GIA	s	Psalm Praise
Hallelujah	Judah L. Wise	SOM	o	
Hallelujah (3x)	Walter Pelz	AUG	o	
Hallelujah!	Shepherd/Pelz	AUG	s	Seasonal Psalms
Jesus Is Life	Carey Landry	NAL	as	Abba, Father
Let Everything That Lives	C. Knoll/F.V. Strahan	HEL	s	The Catholic Liturgy Book
Let The Earth Resound	Lucien Deiss	NAL	ast	Awaken, My Heart
O Praise God	Geoffry Beaumont	GIA	s	Psalm Praise
O Praise God	Norman Gilbert	OXF	o	
O Praise God In His Holiness	Robert White	OXF	o	
O Praise God In His Holiness	William Lovelock	OXF	o	
O Praise God In His Holiness	C. Armstrong Gibbs	OXF		
O Praise God In His Holiness	Charles Stanford	GIA	s	Psalm Praise
O Praise God In His Holiness	Leslie Paul	OXF	o	
O Praise God In His Holiness	Matthew White	OXF	o	
Pilgrim's Earth Psalm	W. Williamson	BOH		
Praise God	Westendorf/Vermulst	WLP	s	People's Mass Book,1984
Praise God For His Mighty	Howard Hughes	GIA	s	Praise God In Song
Praise God From Whom All Blessin	Thomas Ken	CON	s	The Lutheran Hymnal
Praise God From Whom All Blessin	Ken/Bourgeois	AUG	s	Lutheran Book Of Worship
Praise God In His Holy Dwelling	Jan Vermulst	WLP	as	Songs Of Praise,2
Praise God In His Holy Place	Joseph Gelineau	GIA	s	30 Psalms & 2 Canticles
Praise God In His Holy Temple	Carl Crosier	GIA	o	Choral Series,1985
Praise Him	McKay	AUG	o	
Praise The Lord	Austin C. Lovelace	GIA	o	Choral Series,1985
Praise The Lord	Paul Quinlan	NAL	a	Love And Question
Praise The Lord	Dan Schutte	NAL	as	Neither Silver Nor Gold
Praise The Lord	Eugene Englert	GIA	o	
Praise The Lord His Glories	Lyte/Williams	PIL	s	Pilgrim Hymnal
Praise The Lord In His Holy	Joe Wise	PAA	ast	Songs For The Journey
Praise The Lord Who Reigns	Charles Wesley	MPH	s	The Book Of Hymns
Praise The Lord With Blasts	Marivoet/de Sutter	HEL	s	The Catholic Liturgy Book
Praise To The Lord The Almighty	Joachim Neander	HEL	s	The Catholic Liturgy Book

Praise To The Lord, The Almighty	J. Neander	CPF	s	The Hymnal 1940
Praise Ye The Lord	Jean Berger	FLA	o	The Bay Psalm Book
Praise Ye The Lord	John Rutter	OXF	o	
Praise Ye The Lord	Gerhard Track	GIA	o	
Sing Alleluia, Praise The Lord	Becker, Reuning/Schutz	GIA	s	Worship II
With Merry Dancing	Dan Schutte	NAL	as	Neither Silver Nor Gold
With The Lord	M. Joncas	NAL	as	Here In Our Midst
Wondrous King All Praises	J. Neander	CON	s	The Lutheran Hymnal

Responsorial Psalms for the Sundays and Holydays of the Year Roman Catholic Lectionary

Seasonal Psalms

Advent	25,85	Lent	51,91,130
Christmas	98	Easter	66,104,118
Ordinary 1	100,103	Ordinary 2	19,27,34,63,95,145

Sunday or Holyday	Cycle	A	B	C
Advent 1		122	80	25
Advent 2		72	85	126
Advent 3		146	(Lk1)	(Is12)
Advent 4		24	89	80
Christmas Vigil		89	89	89
Christmas Midnight		96	96	96
Christmas Dawn		97	97	97
Christmas Day		98	98	98
Sunday in the Octave of Christmas (Holy Family)		128	128	128
Octave of Christmas (January 1)		67	67	67
Christmas 2		147	147	147
Epiphany		72	72	72
Baptism of the Lord (Epiphany 1)		29	29	29
Lent 1		51	25	91
Lent 2		33	116	27
Lent 3		95	19	103
Lent 4		23	137	34
Lent 5		130	51	126
Passion Sunday		22	22	22
Holy Thursday (Chrism)		89	89	89
Holy Thursday (Lord's Supper)		116	116	116
Good Friday		31	31	31
Easter Vigil		104	104	104
		33	33	33
		16	16	16
		30	30	30
		19	19	19
		42	42	42
		51	51	51
		118	118	118

Easter Sunday	118	118	118
Easter 2	118	118	118
Easter 3	16	4	30
Easter 4	23	118	100
Easter 5	33	22	145
Easter 6	66	98	67
Ascension	47	47	47
Easter 7	27	103	97
Pentecost Vigil	104	104	104
Pentecost Sunday	104	104	104
Sunday 1 after Pentecost (Trinity)	(Dn3)	33	8
Sunday 2	40	40	96
Sunday 3	27	25	19
Sunday 4	146	95	71
Sunday 5	112	147	138
Sunday 6	119	32	1
Sunday 7	103	41	103
Sunday 8	62	103	92
Sunday 9	31	81	117
Sunday 10	50	130	30
Sunday 11	100	92	32
Sunday 12	69	107	63
Sunday 13	89	30	16
Sunday 14	145	123	66
Sunday 15	65	85	69
Sunday 16	86	23	15
Sunday 17	119	145	138
Sunday 18	145	78	95
Sunday 19	85	34	33
Sunday 20	67	34	40
Sunday 21	138	34	117
Sunday 22	63	115	68
Sunday 23	95	146	90
Sunday 24	103	116	51
Sunday 25	145	54	113
Sunday 26	125	19	146
Sunday 27	80	128	95
Sunday 28	23	90	98
Sunday 29	96	33	121
Sunday 30	18	126	34
Sunday 31	131	18	145
Sunday 32	63	146	17
Sunday 33	128	16	98
Last Sunday (Christ the King)	23	93	122
Corpus Christi	147	116	110
Assumption Vigil	132	132	132
Assumption Day (August 15)	45	45	45
All Saints (November 1)	24	24	24
Immaculate Conception (December 8)	98	98	98

Listing of Publishers

ABB   Abbey Press
62 Hill Dr.
St. Meinrad, IN 47577

ABI   Abingdon Music
201 Eighth Ave. So.
Nashville, TN 37202

ACP   American Catholic Press
1223 Rossell Ave.
Oak Park, IL 60302

AGA   Agape (Hope Publishing Co.)
380 So. Main St.
Carol Stream, IL 60187

AHC   Alba House
Canfield, OH 44406

ASA   Asaph Productions
P.O. Box 7972
Fresno, CA 93727

AUG   Augsburg Publishing Co.
426 So. Fifth St.
Minneapolis, MN 55415

BBL   Broude Bros. Ltd.
56 West 45th. St.
New York, NY 10036

BOH   Boosey & Hawkes
P.O. Box 130
Oceanside, NY 11572

CFP   C.F.Peters
373 Park Ave. So.
New York, NY 10016

CFS   Carl Fischer Inc.
56-62 Cooper Square
New York, NY 10003

CHO   Chorister's Guild
P.O. Box 38118
Dallas, TX 75238

CLM   Cherry Lane Music
Box 4247/ 50 Old Post Rd.
Greenwich, CT 06830

CON   Concordia Publishing House
3558 So. Jefferson Ave.
St. Louis, MO 63118

COO   Cooperative Ministries
P.O. Box 4463
Washington, D.C. 20017

CPF   Church Pension Fund
800 Second Ave.
New York, NY 10017

EKK   Ekklesia Music Inc.
3750 So. Hillcrest Dr.
Denver, CO 80237

ERD   Wm. B. Eerdman Publishing Co.
225 Jefferson Ave. SE
Grand Rapids, MI 49502

FCC   Franciscan Communications Ctr.
1229 So. Santee St.
Los Angeles, CA 90015

FEL   FEL Publications
1925 So. Pontius Ave.
Los Angeles, CA 90025

FLA   Harold Flammer
Del Water Gap, PA 18327

GIA   GIA Publications Inc.
7404 So. Mason Ave.
Chicago, IL 60638

GPH   Gospel Publishing House
1445 Boonville Ave.
Springfield, MO 65802

GRA   General Recording/Audio-Visual
235 Sharon Dr.
San Antonio, TX 78216

HEL   Helicon Press
1120 N. Calvert St.
Baltimore, MD 21202

HOP   Hope Publishing Co.
380 So. Main St.
Carol Stream, IL 60187

ICE ICEL Publications
1234 Massachusetts Ave. NW
Washington, DC 20025

MLH Music from Marylhurst
Marylhurst Education Ctr.
Marylhurst, OR 97036

MPH United Methodist Publishing House
201 Eighth Ave. So.
Nashville, TN 37202

NAL No. American Liturgy Resources
2110 West Peoria Ave.
Phoenix, AZ 85029

NOV Novello Publications
145 Palisade St.
Dobbs Ferry, NY 10522

OSB Order of St. Benedict
St. John's University
Collegeville, MN 56321

OXF Oxford University Press
200 Madison Ave.
New York, NY 10016

PAA Pastoral Arts Associates
Old Hickory, TN 37138

PAS Pastorale Music
235 Sharon Dr.
San Antonio, TX 78216

PIL The Pilgrim Press
287 Park Ave. So.
New York, NY 10010

PRE Theodore Presser Co.
Presser Place
Bryn Mawr, PA 19010

PRO Pro Art Publishers Inc.
P.O. Box 234
Westbury, NY 11590

RAV Raven Music
4107 Woodland Park No.
Seattle, WA 98103

RPB Resource Publications Inc.
160 E. Virginia St. #290
San Jose, CA 95112

SFM St. Francis Music
200 Noll Plaza
Huntingdon, IN 46750

SOM Southern Music Publishers
1740 Broadway
New York, NY 10019

TMI Today's Missal Publishing Co.
2816 East Brnside
Portland, OR 97214

WES Weston Priory Productions
Weston, VT 05161

WGM Word of God Music
(Servant Pubs.)
P.O. Box 87
Ann Arbor, MI 48107

WLP World Library Publications
5040 N. Ravenswood
Chicago, IL 60640

WRD Word Inc.
P.O. Box 1790
Waco, TX 76703

Singing the Psalms in Liturgies

Psalms can be sung in a number of ways:
— in responsorial settings in which a cantor, song leader or choir sings the verses and the congregation sings a "one-line" refrain,
— in antiphonal style in which the congregation is divided into two groups which alternate verses,
— in metrical hymn settings,
and
— in paraphrases or songs based on a psalm but not metrical, such as through-composed anthems.

Responsorial settings are the easiest for many parish congregations and are found in practically all service hymnals, liturgical songbooks and missalettes. This style is very versatile; the congregation sings the appointed daily or seasonal response and the cantor, choir, folk group or schola sings the verses using metrical or chant settings. Gelineau, Deiss and others have well-known chant versions and The Dameans, Michael Joncas, Marty Haugen and others have written metrical versions.

Antiphonal psalm singing is more usually found in monastic communities but can be found in musically more advanced parishes. The same psalm tone is used by each of the alternating sides of the congregation, and everybody sings a refrain at the beginning and at the end. This style is better suited to the psalms sung in the Liturgy of the Hours rather than the responsorial of the Eucharistic Liturgy of the Word.

Metrical hymns have a strong tradition and many are well known. They stay close to the original psalm; many may be found in standard church hymnals, e.g. "O God, Our Help In Ages Past," (Psalm 90), "A Mighty Fortress Is Our God," (Psalm 46). These hymns have an important place in the worship tradition of all Christian denominations, but their use in Catholic liturgy would seem to be limited to processionals and special occasions.

In *Music In Catholic Worship* (1983), the Bishops' Committee on the Liturgy states (paragraph 63):

"The liturgy of the Word comes more fully to life if between the first two readings a cantor sings a psalm and all sing the response. Since most groups cannot learn a new response every week, seasonal refrains are offered in the lectionary itself and in the *Simple Gradual*. Other psalms and refrains may also be used, including psalms arranged in responsorial form and metrical and similar versions of psalms, provided they are used in accordance with the principles of the *Simple Gradual* and are selected in harmony with the liturgical season, feast or occasion."

What criteria should one apply in choosing a way of singing the Psalms? The purpose is to allow the psalm to speak for the assembled people, so they should be involved in the singing. Just because a song has been published it does not follow that the liturgist should use it. In *Music In Catholic Worship* three criteria are given for judging the value of a song: musical, liturgical and pastoral. A song should be used only if it is good music, which can only be decided by a competent musician who must not confuse value and style. Classical music and folk music are different styles; each may have high value. Musical taste also demands a cantor or song leader with a voice good enough to be accepted by the congregation, who is also humble and self-effacing so that he or she is hardly noticed by the community. It must be clear that it is the word of God which is being proclaimed in the psalm.

Applying liturgical judgment to the psalms can mean such things as choosing a setting which does not upstage the Gospel. The psalm is not to be the high point of the liturgy of the Word but must enable the community to pray its response to the first reading. Settings will not then be too elaborate; piano, flute, guitar and organ accompaniments when used will need to suit the liturgical mood. The text chosen should be appropriate to the rest of the liturgical celebration.

Pastoral judgment leads one to ask: Does this particular psalm setting enable this congregation, now, of its particular cultural background, education and age, to feel spoken for? What is good in a monastery, convent or seminary may be quite different from what is good in a college campus chapel, in an inner city church or a suburban one. While Gelineau might be ideal for a seminary, and sound beautiful, it might leave a middle-class parish congregation sitting stone-faced. The latter might better relate to Jack Miffleton and Dan Schutte. Different Masses in the same parish may need different settings—the community at a 4:30 pm Mass on Saturday has a different makeup from that at 7:30 am on Sunday, which is different again from that at 11:00 am. Pastoral judgments cannot be made unless you know your people.

Psalms are particularly appropriate as communion processional songs. It has been recorded that in the fourth century many psalm verses were used as eucharistic songs, generally those referring to God feeding his people:

> *Patiently all creatures look to you*
> *to feed them throughout the year;*
> *quick to satisfy every need,*
> *you feed them all with a generous hand.*
>   Psalm 145:15-16 Jerusalem Bible

The unity of those participating in the eucharist can well be expressed in a psalm sung as a communion processional. Psalm 100 is appropriate:

> *Cry out with joy to the Lord, all the earth.*
> *Serve the Lord with gladness.*
> *Come before him, singing for joy.*
> *Know that he, the Lord, is God.*
> *He made us, we belong to him,*
> *We are his people, the sheep of his flock.*
>   The Grail, verses 1-3

A version might be selected which has a simple refrain for the congregation to sing after each verse has been sung by the choir or song leader, so that carrying books or papers is unnecessary during the procession. Psalm 136 is also especially well suited to communion processions.

Through-composed psalm settings can be expressive and prayerful. They can be used as communion meditations (after the procession) and in the Liturgy of the Hours as a change from responsorial and antiphonal versions. Their use will depend on the three criteria mentioned above.

A final point should be made concerning psalm songs. Sometimes more than one literary idea is found in a single numbered psalm, so songs based on the same psalm number may have quite different themes. Reference to the Lectionary can determine which part of a psalm is suggested for a particular occasion.

Seeking God's Name

Christians should turn back again and again to the words of Jesus of Nazareth to learn how to pray.

How did Jesus pray? The gospel tells us that men began to doubt their own prayer when they saw him praying. "Teach us to pray," they asked him and his answer was: "Our Father, who art in heaven, hallowed be thy name..." In another place, we are told that he prayed the psalms— "God, my God, why have you forsaken me?"

The psalms are everything that is in man. Memories, ideas, feelings of every kind collide and crash against each other in the psalms, in a constant altercation between God and no God.

> *What is man that you remember him,*
> *the son of Adam that you care for him?*

says Psalm 8, and Psalm 22 says:

> *I cry by day: my God, and you are silent—*
> *I cry by night and you just let me.*

Again,

> *You have been, O Lord, a safe dwelling place*
> *for us from generation to generation*

and right next to it, in the same psalm (90), jolting and bumping:

> *You make people turn to dust.*
> *You say: it's all over, O children of Adam.*

The world of the psalms is the world in which Jesus lived—the world of Psalm 42:

> *As a hart stretches out for living water,*
> *so do I reach out, God, with all my being toward you.*
> *I thirst for God, for the living God.*
> *When shall I at last stand face to face with God?...*
> *Why do I go about tearing my clothes,*

tormented and humiliated?
My enemies scare me to death,
mortally wounding my body.
Where is that God of yours, I hear them call.
You are my rescuer,
You are my God.

All this and more is contained in Psalm 42, that nervous, neurotic poem full of inner conflict, for and against. It is a prayer that opens passionately, then sinks into inner doubt, then blazes up in a vision of almost cosmic fear and at last finds peace and tranquility. The spirit is gradually purified in this violent movement and the last, tentative word is reached: "You are my God."

Praying, we shall have to turn more and more toward the psalms. In our liturgical prayer, too, we must try to sound the depths of the psalms and match their quality, evoking for each other the world of Israel's prayer.

Praying is speaking God's name, or rather, seeking God's name. "What is your name?" —the eternal question that comes back again after every answer. It is the question asked by Moses who was permitted to meet God as a "difficult friend" and to talk with him "as a man talks with his friend."

Praying is trying to turn that little word "God" into a name that means something to me, to us, now. It is trying to make that hazardous, volatile little word really expressive. You get nowhere if you just say "God." Those three letters—they are just a code, an unknown quantity, a stopgap. You have to make the long journey from "God," a meaningless, boring, empty cliche, to "our God," "my God," "God of the living," a meaningful, personal name full of echoes of his entire history with mankind, if you really want to pray.

A name is not just a word. A person's name is full of history. A person's name—it at once calls to mind facts and experiences, joy and sorrow, misunderstandings. Speaking a friend's name— it reminds me at once of what we have in common, of the depth and the height of our whole relationship, our life together. I have heard people say of a dead person, "When I speak his name, then he really *is* there."

Praying is "blessing," "praising," "giving honor to" God. That is what the psalms call it. Calling God by his name, giving him the chance to be himself, "our God." In Psalm 104, the psalmist begins by naming God:

> *I will call you, God, by your name*
> *as truly as I am alive"*

and then goes on to talk about creation. He drags everything in, going right back to the beginning, when

> *the waters were still above the mountains*

and then we have wild goats leaping in the hills and the grass and plants growing in the fields and then—man, toiling until darkness falls. Swaggering about the whole world like this, the psalmist hits on the track of God's name:

> *All this, God, your very own work—*
> *your wisdom speaks from so many things,*
> *our earth is full of your power of creation.*

Who is God? What is his name? He is what he does to us. He is called "our earth is full of his power of creation." When the Bible prays, the whole of creation is listed and the whole of God's history with man is brought up again. When we pray, with the Bible, we appeal to creation and to the covenant. We call God to mind and remind him who he is and what he has done. What God used to mean for men in the past includes a promise of the future, the promise that he will mean something for us as well, that he will be someone for us.

Huub Oosterhuis, Your Word Is Near
©1968 The Paulist Press

Bibliography

Anderson, Bernhard W. *Out Of The Depths.* Philadelphia: The West-minster Press, 1983. A Bible and this book would make forty days in the desert pass in no time at all. A "must" for serious liturgists.

Anderson, Bernhard W. *Understanding The Old Testament.* New York: Prentice-Hall, 1975. Chapter 16, "The Praises of Israel" refers to the Psalms. Take it to the desert if you have room in your pack.

Bonhoeffer, Dietrich. *Psalms: The Prayer Book Of The Bible.* Min-neapolis: Augsburg Publishing House, 1974. In this very short book, first published in German just before his arrest by the Nazis, Bonhoeffer claims that it is a "short stroll through the Psalter in order to learn to pray a few psalms a bit better." It contains many insights into praying the Psalms which may be useful to those approaching the Psalter for the first time.

Brandt, Leslie F. *Psalms Now.* St. Louis: Concordia Publishing House, 1973. Psalm paraphrases, prayers and meditiations in up-to-date language.

The Common Bible (ecumenical Revised Standard), the *New American,* the *New English* and the *Jerusalem* Bibles all contain introductions to the Psalms, and of course, the Psalms themselves. It is amazing how many different ways there are of translating the Hebrew, and each speaks to a person in a different way. No one version is sufficient for the serious liturgist.

Deiss, Lucien, C.S.Sp. *Spirit And Song Of The New Liturgy.* Cincinnati: World Library Publications, 1976. Chapter 5 is devoted to the respon-sorial psalm, and other chapters discuss psalm use in liturgy.

The Jerome Biblical Commentary. New York: Prentice-Hall, 1968. Chapter 35, by Roland E. Murphy. The Psalms are not easy to unders-tand; they need an understanding of the Hebrew Bible for their apprecia-tion. This book is a way to get it, if you can afford it and have the strength to carry it.

Mahoney, John. *Give Ear, O Lord.* Chicago: Claretian Publications, 1978. A selection of 24 psalms rendered in non-sexist language. Very in-expensive; a bargain.

Oosterhuis, Huub, et al. *Fifty Psalms.* New York: The Seabury Press, 1973. Beautiful translations for personal and public use, made accessible to all. You will hardly miss the other hundred (99?); these seem to say everything.

The Psalms For Modern Man. New York: American Bible Society, 1970. An effective, very readable translation of the Psalter.

The Psalms: Singing Version. New York: Deus Books, Paulist Press, 1968. The Psalter as translated by the Grail in England. The basis of the Gelineau psalms, it includes formula tones for chanting. It also has commentaries on the psalms. Should be used at least sometimes in any congregation. (Uses Septuagint numbering).

Shepherd, Massey H. *A Liturgical Psalter For The Christian Year.* Minneapolis: Augsburg Publishing House. An ecumenical psalter, with suggestions for antiphons. Has useful commentaries.

Sullivan, Francis P. *Lyric Psalms: Half A Psalter.* Washington DC: National Association of Pastoral Musicians, 1983. A powerful set of psalm re-creations that are a joy to read aloud. The author strove to "give musicians a stable pattern to work with, and lectors a floating pattern of accents for vivid delivery, to give readers tight phrases to recall." Make room for these psalms in your desert kit; proclaim them to the stars at night.

Psalms to List?

Any ongoing index needs constant attention to remain current and be of maximun value to its user. The blank lines in this book give you room to add new songs as they are released or as you discover them.

If you would like to share these additions, please copy or remove this page, put the information on it for each psalm you think we should add and send it to *The Psalm Locator*, Resource Publications, Inc., 160 E. Virginia St.#290, San Jose, CA 95112

Psalm No.　Title　　　　Author　　　Publ.　SC　Collection

_____

Resource Publications, Inc.
160 E. Virginia St.#290
San Jose, CA 95112

Name _____
Address _____
City/State/Zip _____

Postscript

We are as you have made us—
we belong heart and soul to this earth.
Keep us in this grace,
make us faithful to your creation
and teach us to recognize,
in gratitude and delight,
that everything that you have done
is good.

Huub Oosterhuis, Your Word Is Near
©1968 The Paulist Press